MW00749401

cupcakes
cheesecakes
cookies

General manager Christine Whiston
Editorial director Susan Tomnay
Creative director Hieu Chi Nguyen
Designer Hannah Blackmore
Senior editor Stephanie Kistner
Food director Pamela Clark
Food editors Fiona Roberts, Cathie Lonnie
Home economists Ariarne Bradshaw,
Belinda Farlow, Miranda Farr, Nicole
Jennings, Elizabeth Macri, Angela Muscat,
Fiona Roberts, Kirrily La Rosa, Rebecca
Squadrito, Kellie-Marie Thomas

Director of sales Brian Cearnes
Marketing manager Bridget Cody
Senior business analyst Rebecca Varela
Operations manager David Scotto
Production manager Victoria Jefferys
International rights enquiries
Laura Bamford lbamford@acpuk.com

ACP Books are published by
ACP Magazines a division of
PBL Media Pty Limited
Publishing director, Women's lifestyle
Pat Ingram
Director of sales, Women's lifestyle
Lynette Phillips
Commercial manager, Women's lifestyle
Seymour Cohen
Marketing director, Women's lifestyle
Matthew Dominello
Public relations manager,
Women's lifestyle Hannah Deveraux
Research director, Women's lifestyle
Justin Stone
PBL Media, Chief executive officer
Ian Law

Produced by ACP Books, Sydney.
Published by ACP Books, a division of ACP Magazines Ltd.
54 Park St, Sydney NSW Australia 2000. GPO Box 4088, Sydney, NSW 2001.
Phone +61 2 9282 8618 Fax +61 2 9267 9438
acpbooks@acpmagazines.com.au www.acpbooks.com.au
Printed by SNP Leefung Printers, China.

Australia Distributed by Network Services, GPO Box 4088, Sydney, NSW 2001.
Phone +61 2 9282 8777 Fax +61 2 9264 3278
networkweb@networkservicescompany.com.au
United Kingdom Distributed by Australian Consolidated Press (UK),
10 Scirocco Close, Moulton Park Office Village, Northampton, NN3 6AP.
Phone +44 1604 642 200 Fax +44 1604 642 300 books@acpuk.com www.acpuk.com
Canada Publishers Group Canada, 559 College Street, Unit 402, Toronto, Ontario M6G 1A9.
Phone (416) 934 9900 or (800) 747 8147 Fax (416) 934 1410 www.pgcbooks.ca
Order Desk & Customer Service, 9050 Shaughnessy Street, Vancouver, BC V6P 6E5.
Phone (800) 663 5714 Fax (800) 565 3770 Customer service@raincoast.com
New Zealand Distributed by Southern Publishers Group, 21 Newton Rd, Newton,
Auckland. Phone +64 9 360 0692 Fax +64 9 360 0695 hub@spg.co.nz
South Africa Distributed by PSD Promotions, 30 Diesel Road Isando, Gauteng
Johannesburg. PO Box 1175, Isando 1600, Gauteng Johannesburg.
Phone +27 11 392 6065/6/7 Fax +27 11 392 6079/80 orders@psdprom.co.za

Clark, Pamela.
Cupcakes cheesecakes cookies: the Australian women's weekly.
ISBN 978-1-86396-749-5
1. Cupcakes. 2. Cheesecakes (Cookery). 3. Cookies. I. Title: Australian women's weekly.
641.8653
© ACP Magazines Ltd 2008
ABN 18 053 273 546

This publication is copyright. No part of it may be reproduced or transmitted
in any form without the written permission of the publishers.

Originally published in three editions:
Cupcakes in 2006, Cheesecakes in 2006 and Cookies in 2007.
First published 2008. Reprinted 2008.

To order books, phone 136 116 (within Australia).
Send recipe enquiries to: recipeenquiries@acpmagazines.com.au

The publishers would like to thank the following for props used in photography
Anasazi Homewares; Crave; DJ's Upholstery & Antiques; Domayne; Husk; Iris & Hazel;
kikki. K; Mondo; Mozi Design; My Island Home; No Chintz; Orson & Blake; Papaya;
Pavillon Christofle; Publisher Textiles; Signature Prints; Space Furniture; Tatti; Tres Fabu;
T2; Top3 by Design; Signature Prints; and Iced Affair for supplying cookie cutters.

Photographers Joshua Dasey, Ian Wallace
Stylist Margot Braddon
Food stylist & food preparation Nicole Jennings

Cover (clockwise from left) Pineapple hibiscus cupcakes, page 102;
Pineapple and coconut cheesecakes, page 174; Pink macaroons, page 302.
Photographer John Paul Urizar
Stylist Margot Braddon
Food preparation Rebecca Squadrito

THE AUSTRALIAN
Women's Weekly

cupcakes
cheesecakes
cookies

acp
books

contents

Nowadays I often serve cupcakes as a dessert – they never fail to charm. They make wonderful individual cakes at a birthday party too – especially if they're personalised for each guest. As for cheesecakes, well they'll never go out of fashion or favour – they're everyone's favourite, whether served at a barbecue or elegant dinner party. Cookies are great with ice-cream for dessert, taken on a picnic, wrapped up as gifts or simply served with coffee.

Pamela Clark

Food Director

cupcakes

These exquisite little cakes are ideal for afternoon tea, as an elegant and chic dessert for a dinner party, or as splendid and original birthday cakes. While it's true they look like little works of art, and a few of them require some cake decorating experience, most of them are not difficult to make.

veryberry cupcakes

Dried berry buttercake
125g butter, softened
½ teaspoon vanilla extract
⅔ cup (150g) caster sugar
2 eggs
1 cup (150g) dried mixed berries
½ cup (70g) slivered almonds
⅔ cup (100g) plain flour
⅓ cup (50g) self-raising flour
¼ cup (60ml) milk
Sugared fruit
150g fresh blueberries
120g fresh raspberries
1 egg white, beaten lightly
2 tablespoons vanilla sugar
Cream cheese frosting
30g butter, softened
80g cream cheese, softened
1½ cups (240g) icing sugar

1 Prepare sugared fruit.
2 Preheat oven to 170°C/150°C fan-forced. Line 6-hole texas (¾ cup/180ml) or 12-hole standard (⅓ cup/80ml) muffin pan with paper cases.
3 Beat butter, extract, sugar and eggs in small bowl with electric mixer until light and fluffy.
4 Stir in fruit and nuts, then sifted flours and milk. Divide mixture among cases; smooth surface.
5 Bake large cakes about 45 minutes, small cakes about 35 minutes. Turn cakes onto wire rack to cool.
6 Make cream cheese frosting.
7 Spread cakes with frosting. Decorate with sugared fruit.

Sugared fruit
Brush each berry lightly with egg white; roll fruit in sugar. Place fruit on baking-paper-lined tray. Leave about 1 hour or until sugar is dry. (See page 350)

Cream cheese frosting
Beat butter and cheese in small bowl with electric mixer until light and fluffy; gradually beat in sifted icing sugar.

pear butterfly cupcakes

Pear and maple buttercake

1 medium fresh pear (230g), grated coarsely

60g butter, softened

¼ cup (35g) self-raising flour

¾ cup (110g) plain flour

1 teaspoon ground cinnamon

½ cup (110g) firmly packed brown sugar

¼ cup (60ml) maple-flavoured syrup

2 eggs

⅓ cup (40g) coarsely chopped pecans

⅓ cup (55g) finely chopped dried pear

Pear butterflies

1 tablespoon caster sugar

1 tablespoon water

1 medium brown pear (230g) (eg. beurre bosc), sliced thinly

Fondant icing

500g white prepared fondant, chopped coarsely

1 egg white

blue, pink and yellow food colouring

1 Make pear butterflies.

2 Preheat oven to 180°C/160°C fan-forced. Line 6-hole texas (¾ cup/180ml) or 12-hole standard (⅓ cup/80ml) muffin pan with paper cases.

3 Drain fresh pear, squeezing out as much juice as possible. You need ⅔ cup grated pear.

4 Beat butter, flours, cinnamon, sugar, syrup and eggs in small bowl with electric mixer on low speed until ingredients are combined. Beat on medium speed until mixture is changed to a paler colour.

5 Stir in fresh pear, nuts and dried pear. Divide mixture among cases; smooth surface.

6 Bake large cakes about 35 minutes, small cakes about 30 minutes. Turn cakes onto wire rack to cool.

7 Make fondant icing. Divide icing into three small bowls; using colourings, tint icing pale blue, pink and yellow. Spoon icing quickly over cakes, level with tops of cases; allow to set.

8 Top cakes with pear slices.

Pear butterflies

Preheat oven to 120°C/100°C fan-forced. Combine sugar and the water in small saucepan. Stir over medium heat, without boiling, until sugar is dissolved. Bring to a boil, reduce heat; simmer, without stirring, 1 minute. Brush pear slices both sides with sugar syrup. Place slices in a single layer on a wire rack over oven tray (see page 351). Dry in oven about 40 minutes. While pears are still warm, shape into butterfly wings (see page 351). Cool on wire rack.

Fondant icing

Place fondant in a medium bowl over a medium saucepan of simmering water; stir until smooth. Stir in egg white. Stand at room temperature for about 10 minutes or until thickened slightly.

Chocolate ginger cake
½ cup (110g) firmly packed
   brown sugar
½ cup (75g) plain flour
½ cup (75g) self-raising flour
¼ teaspoon bicarbonate of soda
1 teaspoon ground ginger
½ teaspoon ground cinnamon
¼ teaspoon ground nutmeg
90g butter, softened
1 egg
¼ cup (60ml) buttermilk
2 tablespoons golden syrup
50g dark eating chocolate,
   chopped coarsely
Decorations
300ml thickened cream
3 x 50g violet crumble bars,
   chopped coarsely

1 Preheat oven to 170°C/150°C fan-forced. Line 6-hole texas (¾ cup/180ml) or 12-hole standard (⅓ cup/80ml) muffin pan with paper cases.
2 Sift dry ingredients into small bowl, add butter, egg, buttermilk and syrup; beat mixture with electric mixer on low speed until ingredients are combined. Increase speed to medium, beat until mixture is changed to a paler colour. Stir in chocolate. Divide mixture among cases; smooth surface.
3 Bake large cakes about 40 minutes, small cakes about 30 minutes. Turn cakes onto wire rack to cool.
4 Spread cakes with whipped cream; top with violet crumble.

honeycomb cream cupcakes

Vanilla buttercake
90g butter, softened
½ teaspoon vanilla extract
½ cup (110g) caster sugar
2 eggs
1 cup (150g) self-raising flour
2 tablespoons milk
Butter cream frosting
125g butter, softened
1½ cups (240g) icing sugar
2 tablespoons milk
50g dark eating chocolate,
   chopped finely
1 tablespoon cocoa powder
pink food colouring
Decorations
ice cream waffle cones
strawberry slices
toasted flaked coconut
finely grated dark eating
   chocolate

1 Preheat oven to 180°C/160°C fan-forced. Line 6-hole texas (¾ cup/180ml) or 12-hole standard (⅓ cup/80ml) muffin pan with paper cases.
2 Beat butter, extract, sugar, eggs, flour and milk in small bowl with electric mixer on low speed until ingredients are just combined. Increase speed to medium, beat until mixture is changed to a paler colour.
3 Divide mixture among cases; smooth surface.
4 Bake large cakes about 25 minutes, small cakes about 20 minutes. Turn cakes onto wire rack to cool.
5 Make butter cream frosting.
6 Remove cases from cakes. Using a serrated knife, shape cakes into balls (see page 350) so they sit inside waffle cones.
7 Place cakes in cones, spread with frosting; decorate with strawberries, coconut and grated chocolate.

Butter cream frosting
Beat butter in small bowl with electric mixer until light and fluffy; beat in sifted icing sugar and milk, in two batches. Divide mixture among four small bowls. Add chopped chocolate to one and sifted cocoa to another. Using colouring, tint one pink and leave one plain.

ice-cream cone cupcakes

Cream cheese lemon cake
90g butter, softened
90g cream cheese, softened
2 teaspoons finely grated
 lemon rind
²⁄₃ cup (150g) caster sugar
2 eggs
¹⁄₃ cup (50g) self-raising flour
½ cup (75g) plain flour
Meringue cases
3 egg whites
¾ cup (165g) caster sugar
1 tablespoon cornflour
1 teaspoon white vinegar
½ teaspoon vanilla extract
Decorations
300ml thickened cream,
 whipped
125g strawberries, quartered
1 tablespoon passionfruit pulp
½ cup (75g) blueberries
1 medium banana (230g),
 sliced thickly

1 Make meringue cases.
2 Preheat oven to 180°C/160°C
fan-forced. Line 6-hole texas
(¾ cup/180ml) or 12-hole standard
(¹⁄₃ cup/80ml) muffin pan with
paper cases.
3 Beat butter, cheese, rind,
sugar and eggs in small bowl
with electric mixer until light
and fluffy.
4 Add flours to cheese mixture;
beat on low speed until
combined. Divide mixture
among cases; smooth surface.
5 Bake large cakes about
30 minutes, small cakes about
20 minutes. Turn cakes onto
wire rack to cool.
6 Drop a teaspoon of whipped
cream on each cake; top with
meringue cases. Spoon
remaining cream into cases
and decorate with fruit.

Meringue cases
Preheat oven to 120°C/100°C
fan-forced. Grease oven tray;
line base with baking paper,
trace six 8.5cm circles onto
paper for large cakes, and
12 x 5.5cm circles for small
cakes. Beat egg whites in small
bowl with electric mixer until
soft peaks form. Gradually add
sugar, a tablespoon at a time,
beating until sugar dissolves
between additions. Fold in
cornflour, vinegar and extract.
Spoon meringue inside circles
on tray; hollow out slightly. Bake
45 minutes or until cases are firm.
Cool in oven with door ajar.

lemon pavlova cupcakes

choc-mint mousse cupcakes

Double chocolate mint cake
125g box (16) square after dinner mints
60g dark eating chocolate, chopped coarsely
⅔ cup (160ml) water
90g butter, softened
½ teaspoon peppermint essence
1 cup (220g) firmly packed brown sugar
2 eggs
⅔ cup (100g) self-raising flour
2 tablespoons cocoa powder
⅓ cup (40g) almond meal
1 tablespoon cocoa powder, extra

Chocolate mousse
150g dark eating chocolate, chopped roughly
½ teaspoon peppermint essence
¾ cup (180ml) thickened cream
2 eggs, separated
2 tablespoons caster sugar

1 Make chocolate mousse.
2 Preheat oven to 170°C/150°C fan-forced. Line 6-hole texas (¾ cup/180ml) or 12-hole standard (⅓ cup/80ml) muffin pan with paper cases.
3 For large cakes, using a 3.5cm long petal cutter, cut out 2 petals from each after dinner mint. For small cakes use a 1cm long petal cutter, to cut 4 petals from each after dinner mint. Coarsely chop off-cuts, reserve for cake mixture.
4 Combine chocolate and the water in small saucepan; stir over low heat until smooth.
5 Beat butter, essence, sugar and eggs in small bowl with electric mixer until light and fluffy.
6 Stir in sifted flour and cocoa, almond meal, warm chocolate mixture and reserved after dinner mints. Divide mixture among cases; smooth surface.
7 Bake large cakes about 40 minutes, small cakes about 30 minutes. Turn cakes onto wire rack to cool.

8 Place a lightly greased collar of foil around each cake. Divide firm chocolate mousse evenly among tops of cakes. Freeze cakes for about 30 minutes to help set the mousse quickly.
9 Dust mousse with extra sifted cocoa; arrange petals on top in a flower. Gently remove foil; dip spatula in hot water and smooth side of mousse.

Chocolate mousse
Combine chocolate, essence and half the cream in a medium heatproof bowl over a medium saucepan of simmering water; stir until smooth. Cool mixture 5 minutes, then stir in egg yolks. Beat remaining cream in small bowl with electric mixer until soft peaks form. Beat egg whites in another small bowl with electric mixer until soft peaks form; add sugar gradually, beat until dissolved. Fold cream into chocolate mixture, then egg whites. Spoon mixture into a shallow baking dish. Cover; refrigerate 4 hours or until firm.

sugar & lace cupcakes

Caramel mud cake
125g butter, chopped coarsely
100g white eating chocolate,
 chopped coarsely
⅔ cup (150g) firmly packed
 brown sugar
¼ cup (90g) golden syrup
⅔ cup (160ml) milk
1 cup (150g) plain flour
⅓ cup (50g) self-raising flour
1 egg
Decorations
doily, lace or stencil
½ cup (80g) icing sugar

1 Preheat oven to 170°C/150°C fan-forced. Line 6-hole texas (¾ cup/180ml) or 12-hole standard (⅓ cup/80ml) muffin pan with paper cases.
2 Combine butter, chocolate, sugar, syrup and milk in small saucepan; stir over low heat, until smooth. Transfer mixture to medium bowl; cool 15 minutes.
3 Whisk sifted flours into chocolate mixture, then egg. Divide mixture among cases.
4 Bake large cakes about 40 minutes, small cakes about 30 minutes. Turn cakes onto wire rack to cool.
5 Place doily, lace or stencil over cake; sift a little icing sugar over doily (see page 350), then carefully lift doily from cake. Repeat with remaining cakes and icing sugar.

cloud cupcakes

Strawberry swirl buttercake
90g butter, softened
½ teaspoon vanilla extract
½ cup (110g) caster sugar
2 eggs
1 cup (150g) self-raising flour
2 tablespoons milk
2 tablespoons strawberry jam
Fluffy frosting
1 cup (220g) caster sugar
⅓ cup (80ml) water
2 egg whites
Decorations
pink coloured sugar
   (see page 351)

1 Preheat oven to (180°C/160°C fan-forced. Line 6-hole texas (¾ cup/180ml) or 12-hole standard (⅓ cup/80ml) muffin pan with paper cases.
2 Beat butter, extract, sugar, eggs, flour and milk in small bowl with electric mixer on low speed until ingredients are just combined. Increase speed to medium, beat until mixture is changed to a paler colour.
3 Divide mixture among cases; smooth surface. Divide jam over tops of cakes; using a skewer swirl jam into cakes.
4 Bake large cakes about 30 minutes, small cakes about 20 minutes. Turn cakes onto wire rack to cool.
5 Make fluffy frosting.
6 Spread cakes with fluffy frosting; sprinkle with coloured sugar.

Fluffy frosting
Combine sugar and the water in small saucepan; stir over heat, without boiling, until sugar is dissolved. Boil, uncovered, without stirring about 5 minutes or until syrup reaches 116°C on a candy thermometer. Syrup should be thick but not coloured. Remove from heat, allow bubbles to subside. Beat egg whites in small bowl with electric mixer until soft peaks form. While mixer is operating, add hot syrup in thin stream; beat on high speed about 10 minutes or until mixture is thick and cool.

toffee-apple tower cupcakes

Maple, pecan and apple cake
60g butter, softened
1 cup (150g) self-raising flour
1 teaspoon ground cinnamon
½ cup (110g) firmly packed
 brown sugar
¼ cup (60ml) maple-flavoured
 syrup
2 eggs
⅔ cup (80g) coarsely chopped
 pecans
½ cup (85g) coarsely grated
 apple
Maple frosting
90g butter, softened
1 cup (160g) icing sugar
2 teaspoons maple-flavoured
 syrup
Toffee
1 cup (220g) caster sugar
½ cup (125ml) water

1 Preheat oven to 180°C/160°C
fan-forced. Line 6-hole texas
(¾ cup/180ml) or 12-hole standard
(⅓ cup/80ml) muffin pan with
paper cases.
2 Beat butter, flour, cinnamon,
sugar, syrup and eggs in small
bowl with electric mixer on low
speed until ingredients are
combined. Increase speed to
medium, beat until mixture is
changed to a paler colour.
3 Stir in nuts and grated apple.
Divide mixture among cases;
smooth surface.
4 Bake large cakes about
35 minutes, small cakes about
25 minutes. Turn cakes onto
wire rack to cool.
5 Make maple frosting.
Make toffee.
6 Spread cakes with frosting;
decorate with toffee shards.

Maple frosting
Beat butter, sifted icing sugar and
syrup in small bowl with electric
mixer until light and fluffy.

Toffee
Combine sugar with the water
in small heavy-based saucepan.
Stir over heat, without boiling,
until sugar dissolves; bring to
the boil. Reduce heat; simmer,
uncovered, without stirring,
until mixture is golden brown.
Remove from heat; stand until
bubbles subside. Make toffee
shards on baking-paper-lined
oven tray (see page 345).

turkish delight cupcakes

White chocolate pistachio cake

60g white eating chocolate,
  chopped roughly
2 tablespoons rose water
½ cup (125ml) water
⅓ cup (45g) pistachio nuts
90g butter, softened
1 cup (220g) firmly packed
  brown sugar
2 eggs
⅔ cup (100g) self-raising flour
2 tablespoons plain flour

Decorations

⅔ cup (90g) coarsely chopped
  pistachio nuts
300g white eating chocolate,
  melted
900g turkish delight, chopped

1 Preheat oven to 180°C/160°C fan-forced. Line 6-hole texas (¾ cup/180ml) or 12-hole standard (⅓ cup/80ml) muffin pan with paper cases.

2 Combine chocolate, rose water and the water in small saucepan; stir over low heat until smooth.

3 Blend or process nuts until fine.

4 Beat butter, sugar and eggs in small bowl with electric mixer until combined.

5 Fold in sifted flours, ground pistachios and warm chocolate mixture. Divide among cases.

6 Bake large cakes about 35 minutes, small cakes about 25 minutes. Turn cakes onto wire rack to cool.

7 Cut a 3cm deep hole in the centre of each cake; fill with a few chopped nuts. Drizzle with a little chocolate; replace lids.

8 Decorate cakes with pieces of turkish delight and chopped nuts dipped in chocolate.

rocky road cupcakes

Marble cake
125g butter, softened
½ teaspoon vanilla extract
⅔ cup (150g) caster sugar
2 eggs
1¼ cups (185g) self-raising flour
⅓ cup (80ml) milk
pink food colouring
1 tablespoon cocoa powder
2 teaspoons milk, extra

Rocky road topping
½ cup (70g) unsalted roasted
  peanuts
1 cup (200g) red glacé cherries,
  halved
1 cup (100g) pink and white
  marshmallows, chopped
  coarsely
½ cup (25g) flaked coconut,
  toasted
200g milk eating chocolate,
  melted

Decorations
50g milk chocolate Melts,
  melted

1 Preheat oven to 180°C/160°C fan-forced. Line 6-hole texas (¾ cup/180ml) or 12-hole standard (⅓ cup/80ml) muffin pan with paper cases.

2 Beat butter, extract, sugar and eggs in small bowl with electric mixer until light and fluffy. Stir in sifted flour and milk in two batches.

3 Divide mixture evenly among three bowls. Tint one mixture pink. Blend sifted cocoa with extra milk in cup; stir into another mixture. Leave third mixture plain.

4 Drop alternate spoonfuls of the mixtures into cases. Pull a skewer backwards and forwards through mixtures for a marbled effect; smooth surface.

5 Bake large cakes about 30 minutes, small cakes about 20 minutes. Turn cakes onto wire rack to cool.

6 Combine ingredients for rocky road topping in medium bowl.

7 Place topping on tops of cakes; drizzle with chocolate.

lamington angel cupcakes

Vanilla buttercake
90g butter, softened
½ teaspoon vanilla extract
½ cup (110g) caster sugar
2 eggs
1 cup (150g) self-raising flour
2 tablespoons milk

Chocolate icing
10g butter
⅓ cup (80ml) milk
2 cups (320g) icing sugar
¼ cup (25g) cocoa powder

Decorations
1 cup (80g) desiccated coconut
¼ cup (100g) raspberry jam
½ cup (125ml) thickened cream,
  whipped

1 Preheat oven to 180°C/160°C fan-forced. Line 6-hole texas (¾ cup/180ml) or 12-hole standard (⅓ cup/80ml) muffin pan with paper cases.
2 Beat butter, extract, sugar, eggs, flour and milk in small bowl with electric mixer on low speed until ingredients are just combined. Increase speed to medium, beat until mixture is changed to a paler colour.
3 Divide mixture among cases; smooth surface.
4 Bake large cakes about 25 minutes, small cakes about 20 minutes. Turn cakes onto wire rack to cool.
5 Make chocolate icing.
6 Remove cases from cakes. Dip cakes in icing; drain off excess, toss cakes in coconut. Place cakes on wire rack to set.
7 Cut cakes as desired; fill with jam and cream.

Chocolate icing
Melt butter in medium heatproof bowl over medium saucepan of simmering water. Stir in milk and sifted icing sugar and cocoa until icing is a coating consistency.

Ginger buttermilk cake
½ cup (110g) firmly packed brown sugar
½ cup (75g) plain flour
½ cup (75g) self-raising flour
¼ teaspoon bicarbonate of soda
1 teaspoon ground ginger
½ teaspoon ground cinnamon
¼ teaspoon ground nutmeg
90g butter, softened
1 egg
¼ cup (60ml) buttermilk
2 tablespoons golden syrup
Decorations
½ cup (80g) icing sugar
400g white prepared fondant
⅓ cup (110g) ginger marmalade, warmed, strained
50g red prepared fondant
50g black prepared fondant

1 Preheat oven to 170°C/150°C fan-forced. Line 6-hole texas (¾ cup/180ml) or 12-hole standard (⅓ cup/80ml) muffin pan with paper cases.
2 Sift dry ingredients into small bowl, then add remaining ingredients. Beat mixture with electric mixer on low speed until ingredients are combined. Increase speed to medium, beat until mixture is changed to a paler colour.
3 Divide mixture among cases; smooth surface.
4 Bake large cakes about 40 minutes, small cakes about 30 minutes. Turn cakes onto wire rack to cool.
5 Dust surface with sifted icing sugar; knead white prepared fondant until smooth. Roll out fondant to a thickness of 5mm. Cut out rounds large enough to cover tops of cakes.

6 Brush tops of cakes with marmalade; cover with fondant rounds (see page 346).
7 Roll out red and black fondants, separately, until 5mm thick. Cut out shapes using heart, diamond, club and spade cutter.
8 Roll out red and black fondant scraps, separately, to a thickness of 2mm. Cut out 'A's using an alphabet cutter set.
9 Secure fondant shapes to cakes by brushing backs with a tiny amount of water.

sweet ginger cupcake aces

coconut cupcake kisses

White chocolate mud cake
125g butter, chopped coarsely
80g white eating chocolate,
    chopped coarsely
1 cup (220g) caster sugar
½ cup (125ml) milk
½ cup (75g) plain flour
½ cup (75g) self-raising flour
½ teaspoon coconut essence
1 egg
**Whipped white
chocolate ganache**
¼ cup (60ml) cream
185g white eating chocolate,
    chopped coarsely
1 tablespoon coconut liqueur
Decorations
3 x 150g boxes ferrero raffaelo
    chocolate truffles

1 Preheat oven to 170°C/150°C fan-forced. Line 6-hole texas (¾ cup/180ml) or 12-hole standard (⅓ cup/80ml) muffin pan with paper cases.
2 Combine butter, chocolate, sugar and milk in small saucepan; stir over low heat until smooth. Transfer mixture to medium bowl; cool 15 minutes.
3 Whisk in sifted flours, then essence and egg. Divide mixture among cases; smooth surface.
4 Bake large cakes about 40 minutes, small cakes about 30 minutes. Turn cakes onto wire rack to cool.
5 Make whipped white chocolate ganache.
6 Spread cakes with ganache. Top with halved truffles, then stack with whole truffles using a little ganache to secure.

**Whipped white
chocolate ganache**
Bring cream to a boil in small saucepan; pour over chocolate and liqueur in small bowl of electric mixer, stir until smooth. Cover; refrigerate 30 minutes. Beat with an electric mixer until light and fluffy.

froufrou cupcakes

Raspberry coconut cake
125g butter, softened
1 cup (220g) caster sugar
3 eggs
½ cup (75g) plain flour
¼ cup (35g) self-raising flour
½ cup (40g) desiccated coconut
⅓ cup (80g) sour cream
150g frozen raspberries
Cream cheese frosting
60g butter, softened
160g cream cheese, softened
2 teaspoons coconut essence
3 cups (480g) icing sugar
Decorations
1 cup (50g) flaked coconut,
   toasted
15 fresh raspberries, halved

1 Preheat oven to 180°C/160°C fan-forced. Line 6-hole texas (¾ cup/180ml) or 12-hole standard (⅓ cup/80ml) muffin pan with paper cases.
2 Beat butter, sugar and eggs in small bowl with electric mixer until light and fluffy.
3 Stir in sifted flours, coconut, cream and frozen raspberries. Divide mixture among cases; smooth surface.
4 Bake large cakes about 50 minutes, small cakes about 40 minutes. Turn cakes onto wire rack to cool.
5 Make cream cheese frosting.
6 Remove cases from cakes; spread cakes with frosting.
7 Decorate cakes with coconut and raspberries.

Cream cheese frosting
Beat butter, cream cheese and essence in small bowl with electric mixer until light and fluffy; gradually beat in sifted icing sugar.

mochaccino cupcakes

You will need six 350ml or twelve 125ml capacity coffee cups for this recipe.

Mocha mud cake
165g butter, chopped coarsely
100g dark eating chocolate, chopped coarsely
1⅓ cups (290g) caster sugar
⅔ cup (170ml) water
¼ cup (60ml) coffee liqueur
2 tablespoons instant coffee granules
1 cup (150g) plain flour
2 tablespoons self-raising flour
2 tablespoons cocoa powder
1 egg

Decorations
300ml carton thickened cream, whipped
2 tablespoons chocolate-flavoured topping
1 tablespoon cocoa powder

1 Preheat oven to 170°C/150°C fan-forced. Line 6-hole texas (¾ cup/180ml) or 12-hole standard (⅓ cup/80ml) muffin pan with paper cases.

2 Combine butter, chocolate, sugar, the water, liqueur and coffee in small saucepan; stir over low heat until smooth.

3 Transfer mixture to medium bowl; cool 15 minutes. Whisk in sifted flours and cocoa, then egg. Divide mixture among cases.

4 Bake large cakes about 1 hour, small cakes about 50 minutes. Turn cakes onto wire rack to cool.

5 Remove cases from cakes. Place cakes in coffee cups, top with cream. Place chocolate topping into piping bag fitted with small plain tube, pipe spirals over cream; feather and fan cakes by pulling a skewer through the spirals (see page 350) or, dust cakes with sifted cocoa.

life's a beach at 30

We used scrap booking decorations available from craft shops and some newsagents. This cake can be assembled directly onto a table or covered 60cm square cake board.

Lime coconut cake
250g butter, softened
2 teaspoons coconut essence
1 tablespoon finely grated
    lime rind
1⅓ cups (290g) caster sugar
4 eggs
⅔ cup (160ml) milk
1½ cups (120g) desiccated
    coconut
2½ cups (375g) self-raising flour
Coconut cream cheese frosting
60g butter, softened
160g cream cheese, softened
2 teaspoons coconut essence
3 cups (480g) icing sugar
Decorations
60g plain sweet biscuits,
    crushed finely
beach-themed decorations

1 Preheat oven to 180°C/160°C fan-forced. Line two 12-hole standard (⅓ cup/80ml) muffin pans with paper cases.
2 Beat butter, essence, rind, sugar and eggs in large bowl with electric mixer until combined.
3 Stir in milk and coconut, then sifted flour. Divide mixture among cases; smooth surface.
4 Bake cakes about 25 minutes. Turn cakes onto wire rack to cool.
5 Make coconut cream cheese frosting.
6 Cover backs of decorations with baking paper to prevent them staining.
7 Spread cakes with frosting; dip tops of cakes into biscuit crumbs, top with decorations.

Coconut cream cheese frosting
Beat butter, cream cheese and essence in small bowl with electric mixer until light and fluffy; gradually beat in sifted icing sugar.

florentine cupcakes

Double chocolate mud cake
60g dark eating chocolate, chopped coarsely
⅔ cup (160ml) water
90g butter, softened
1 cup (220g) firmly packed brown sugar
2 eggs
⅔ cup (100g) self-raising flour
2 tablespoons cocoa powder
⅓ cup (40g) almond meal

Milk chocolate ganache
100g milk eating chocolate, chopped coarsely
¼ cup (60ml) cream

Florentine topping
1 cup (80g) flaked almonds, toasted
½ cup (115g) coarsely chopped glacé ginger
1 cup (200g) red glacé cherries, halved

Decorations
50g dark eating chocolate, melted

1 Preheat oven to 170°C/150°C fan-forced. Line 6-hole texas (¾ cup/180ml) or 12-hole standard (⅓ cup/80ml) muffin pan with paper cases.
2 Combine chocolate and the water in small saucepan; stir over low heat until smooth.
3 Beat butter, sugar and eggs in small bowl with electric mixer until light and fluffy.
4 Stir in sifted flour and cocoa, almond meal and warm chocolate mixture. Divide mixture among cases; smooth surface.
5 Bake large cakes about 35 minutes, small cakes about 25 minutes. Turn cakes onto wire rack to cool.
6 Make milk chocolate ganache.
7 Combine ingredients for florentine topping in small bowl.
8 Spread cakes with ganache, top with florentine mixture; drizzle with chocolate.

Milk chocolate ganache
Bring cream to a boil in small saucepan, pour over chocolate in small bowl; stir until smooth. Stand at room temperature until ganache is spreadable.

baby blue cupcakes

Choc-orange almond cake
60g dark eating chocolate,
   chopped coarsely
1 teaspoon finely grated
   orange rind
⅔ cup (160ml) orange juice
90g butter, softened
1 cup (220g) firmly packed
   brown sugar
2 eggs
⅔ cup (100g) self-raising flour
2 tablespoons cocoa powder
⅓ cup (40g) almond meal
Decorations
½ cup (80g) icing sugar
400g white prepared fondant
blue food colouring
⅓ cup (110g) orange marmalade,
   warmed, strained
2m ribbon, approximately

1 Preheat oven to 170°C/150°C
fan-forced. Line 6-hole texas
(¾ cup/180ml) or 12-hole standard
(⅓ cup/80ml) muffin pan with
paper cases.
2 Combine chocolate, rind and
juice in small saucepan; stir over
low heat until smooth.
3 Beat butter, sugar and eggs
in small bowl with electric mixer
until light and fluffy.
4 Stir in sifted flour and cocoa,
almond meal and warm
chocolate mixture. Divide
mixture among cases; smooth
surface.
5 Bake large cakes about
35 minutes, small cakes about
25 minutes. Turn cakes onto
wire rack to cool.
6 Dust surface with sifted icing
sugar, knead fondant until
smooth. Knead blue colouring
into fondant (see page 346).
7 Brush tops of cakes with
marmalade. Roll fondant out to
5mm thickness; cut rounds large
enough to cover tops of cakes.
8 Place rounds on cakes; tie
cakes with ribbon.

tiramisu cupcakes

Vanilla buttercake
90g butter, softened
½ teaspoon vanilla extract
½ cup (110g) caster sugar
2 eggs
1 cup (150g) self-raising flour
2 tablespoons milk
Mascarpone cream
250g mascarpone cheese
¼ cup (40g) icing sugar
1 tablespoon marsala
¾ cup (180ml) thickened cream,
    whipped
Coffee mixture
1 tablespoon instant coffee
    granules
⅓ cup (80ml) boiling water
2 tablespoons marsala
Decorations
50g dark eating chocolate,
    grated finely

1 Preheat oven to 180°C/160°C fan-forced. Line 6-hole texas (¾ cup/180ml) or 12-hole standard (⅓ cup/80ml) muffin pan with paper cases.
2 Beat butter, extract, sugar, eggs, flour and milk in small bowl with electric mixer on low speed until ingredients are just combined. Increase speed to medium, beat until mixture is changed to a paler colour. Divide mixture among cases; smooth surface.
3 Bake large cakes about 25 minutes, small cakes about 20 minutes. Turn cakes onto wire rack to cool.
4 Make mascarpone cream. Make coffee mixture.
5 Remove cases from cakes. Cut each cake horizontally into four. Brush both sides of cake slices with coffee mixture. Join cake slices with mascarpone cream.
6 Spread tops of cakes with mascarpone cream; sprinkle with grated chocolate. Refrigerate for 3 hours before serving.

Mascarpone cream
Combine mascarpone, sifted icing sugar and marsala in small bowl; fold in cream.

Coffee mixture
Combine coffee, the water and marsala in small bowl; cool.

Lemon cheesecake

100g plain sweet biscuits

50g butter, melted

2 x 250g packets cream cheese, softened

2 teaspoons finely grated lemon rind

½ cup (110g) caster sugar

2 eggs

Glaze

⅔ cup (220g) apricot jam

2 tablespoons brandy

1 Preheat oven to 150°C/ 130°C fan-forced. Line 6-hole texas (¾ cup/180ml) or 12-hole standard (⅓ cup/80ml) muffin pan with paper cases.

2 Blend or process biscuits until fine. Add butter; process until just combined. Divide mixture among cases; press firmly. Refrigerate 30 minutes.

3 Beat cheese, rind and sugar in small bowl with electric mixer until smooth. Beat in eggs. Pour mixture into cases.

4 Bake large cakes about 30 minutes, small cakes about 25 minutes. Cool.

5 Make glaze.

6 Pour glaze evenly over tops of cheesecakes; refrigerate 2 hours or until glaze is set.

Glaze

Heat jam and brandy in small saucepan over low heat; strain.

lemon cheesecake cupcakes

Fig, caramel and walnut cake
125g butter, softened
½ teaspoon vanilla extract
⅔ cup (150g) caster sugar
2 eggs
¾ cup (150g) finely chopped
   dried figs
½ cup (60g) finely chopped
   walnuts
⅔ cup (100g) plain flour
⅓ cup (50g) self-raising flour
60g Mars bar, chopped finely
¼ cup (60ml) milk
Whipped milk
chocolate ganache
⅓ cup (80ml) cream
200g milk eating chocolate
Toffee
½ cup (110g) caster sugar
¼ cup (60ml) water
Decorations
6 medium fresh figs (360g),
   quartered

1 Preheat oven to 180°C/160°C fan-forced. Line 6-hole texas (¾ cup/180ml) or 12-hole standard (⅓ cup/80ml) muffin pan with paper cases.
2 Beat butter, extract, sugar and eggs in small bowl with electric mixer until light and fluffy.
3 Stir in figs, nuts, sifted flours, mars bar and milk. Divide mixture among cases; smooth surface.
4 Bake large cakes about 40 minutes, small cakes about 30 minutes. Turn cakes onto wire rack to cool.
5 Make whipped milk chocolate ganache.
6 Make toffee; form into shapes over rolling pin (see page 345).
7 Spread cakes with ganache; decorate with fig quarters and toffee shapes.

Whipped milk
chocolate ganache
Bring cream to a boil in small saucepan, pour over chocolate in small bowl of electric mixer, stir until smooth. Cover, refrigerate for 30 minutes. Beat with electric mixer until light and fluffy.

Toffee
Combine sugar with the water in small heavy-based saucepan. Stir over heat, without boiling, until sugar dissolves; bring to the boil. Reduce heat; simmer, uncovered, without stirring, until mixture is golden brown. Remove from heat; stand until bubbles subside.

fig and toffee cupcake crowns

orange blossom cupcakes

Orange, almond and cranberry cake

125g butter, softened
2 teaspoons finely grated orange rind
⅔ cup (150g) caster sugar
2 eggs
1 cup (150g) self-raising flour
⅓ cup (50g) plain flour
⅓ cup (40g) almond meal
½ cup (65g) dried cranberries
¼ cup (60ml) orange juice
2 tablespoons milk

Modelling fondant

2 teaspoons gelatine
1½ tablespoons water
2 teaspoons glucose syrup
1½ cups (240g) pure icing sugar
½ cup (80g) pure icing sugar, extra
yellow, orange and pink food colouring

Butter cream

90g butter, softened
¼ teaspoon orange essence
1 cup (160g) icing sugar
1 tablespoon milk
yellow, orange and pink food colouring

1 Make modelling fondant; reserve a walnut-sized portion.
2 Dust surface with pure icing sugar, roll remaining fondant to a thickness of approximately 3mm. Cut out 18 flowers using 3cm cutter or 36 flowers using 2cm cutter.
3 Divide reserved fondant into three; knead one of the colourings into each portion. Roll tiny balls for flower centres; lightly brush flower centres with water to secure coloured balls.
4 Preheat oven to 180°C/160°C fan-forced. Line 6-hole texas (¾ cup/180ml) or 12-hole standard (⅓ cup/80ml) muffin pan with paper cases.
5 Beat butter, rind, sugar and eggs in small bowl with electric mixer until light and fluffy.
6 Stir in sifted flours, almond meal, cranberries, juice and milk. Divide mixture among cases; smooth surface.
7 Bake large cakes about 35 minutes, small cakes about 25 minutes. Turn cakes onto wire rack to cool.
8 Make butter cream.
9 Spread cakes with butter cream; decorate with flowers.

Modelling fondant
Sprinkle gelatine over the water in cup; stand cup in small saucepan of simmering water, stirring until gelatine is dissolved, add glucose. Place half the sifted icing sugar in small bowl, stir in gelatine mixture. Gradually stir in remaining sifted icing sugar, knead on surface dusted with extra sifted icing sugar until smooth. Enclose in plastic wrap.

Butter cream
Beat butter and essence in small bowl with electric mixer until light and fluffy. Beat in sifted icing sugar and milk, in two batches. Beat in a little of the desired colouring.

neapolitan cupcakes

Marbled buttercake
125g butter, softened
½ teaspoon vanilla extract
⅔ cup (150g) caster sugar
2 eggs
1¼ cups (185g) self-raising flour
⅓ cup (80ml) milk
pink food colouring
1 tablespoon cocoa powder
2 teaspoons milk, extra

Butter cream
125g butter, softened
1½ cups (240g) icing sugar
2 tablespoons milk
pink food colouring
1 tablespoon cocoa powder
2 teaspoons milk, extra

1 Preheat oven to 180°C/160°C fan-forced. Line 6-hole texas (¾ cup/180ml) or 12-hole standard (⅓ cup/80ml) muffin pan with paper cases.
2 Beat butter, extract, sugar and eggs in small bowl with electric mixer until light and fluffy. Stir in sifted flour and milk, in two batches.
3 Divide mixture evenly among three bowls. Tint one mixture pink. Blend sifted cocoa with extra milk in cup; stir into another mixture. Leave third mixture plain.
4 Drop alternate spoonfuls of the three mixtures into cases. Pull a skewer backwards and forwards through mixtures for a marbled effect; smooth surface.
5 Bake large cakes about 30 minutes, small cakes about 20 minutes. Turn cakes onto wire rack to cool.
6 Make butter cream.
7 Spread cakes with the three colours of butter cream.

Butter cream
Beat butter in small bowl with electric mixer until as white as possible; beat in sifted icing sugar and milk, in two batches. Divide mixture evenly among three bowls. Tint one mixture pink. Blend sifted cocoa with extra milk in cup; stir into another mixture. Leave third mixture plain.

kaleidocakes

Orange buttercake
90g butter, softened
90g cream cheese, softened
2 teaspoons finely grated
   orange rind
⅔ cup (150g) caster sugar
2 eggs
⅓ cup (50g) self-raising flour
½ cup (75g) plain flour
Fondant icing
300g white prepared fondant,
   chopped coarsely
1 egg white
¼ teaspoon orange essence
Royal icing
1½ cups (240g) pure icing sugar
1 egg white
½ teaspoon lemon juice
yellow, orange, green, pink and
   purple food colouring

1 Preheat oven to 180°C/160°C fan-forced. Line 6-hole texas (¾ cup/180ml) or 12-hole standard (⅓ cup/80ml) muffin pan with paper cases.
2 Beat butter, cheese, rind, sugar and eggs in small bowl with electric mixer until light and fluffy.
3 Beat in flours on low speed until just combined. Divide mixture among cases; smooth surface.
4 Bake large cakes about 30 minutes, small cakes about 20 minutes. Turn cakes onto wire rack to cool.
5 Make fondant icing. Spread over cakes; allow to set at room temperature.
6 Make royal icing. Divide evenly among five small bowls. Using colourings, tint icing yellow, orange, green, pink and purple; cover each tightly with plastic wrap. Pipe patterns (see page 348) using picture as a guide.

Fondant icing
Place icing in a small bowl over a small saucepan of simmering water; stir until smooth. Stir in egg white and essence. Stand at room temperature for 10 minutes or until thickened slightly. Spread fondant quickly over cakes; use a metal spatula dipped in hot water to smooth surface.

Royal icing
Sift icing sugar through very fine sieve. Lightly beat egg white in small bowl with electric mixer; add icing sugar, a tablespoon at a time. When icing reaches firm peaks, use a wooden spoon to beat in juice; cover tightly with plastic wrap.

banana caramel cupcakes

Sour cream banana cake
90g butter, softened
½ cup (110g) firmly packed
   brown sugar
2 eggs
½ cup (75g) self-raising flour
½ cup (75g) plain flour
½ teaspoon bicarbonate
   of soda
½ teaspoon mixed spice
⅔ cup mashed overripe banana
⅓ cup (80g) sour cream
2 tablespoons milk

Filling and decorations
380g can top 'n' fill caramel
½ cup (125ml) thickened cream,
   whipped
2 medium bananas (400g),
   sliced thinly
100g dark eating chocolate

1 Preheat oven to 180°C/160°C fan-forced. Line 6-hole texas (¾ cup/180ml) or 12-hole standard (⅓ cup/80ml) muffin pan with paper cases.

2 Beat butter, sugar and eggs in small bowl with electric mixer until light and fluffy.

3 Stir in sifted dry ingredients, banana, sour cream and milk. Divide mixture among cases; smooth surface.

4 Bake large cakes about 25 minutes, small cakes about 20 minutes. Turn cakes onto wire rack to cool.

5 Remove cases from cakes.

6 Fold 2 tablespoons of the caramel into cream.

7 Cut cakes horizontally into three slices. Re-assemble cakes with remaining caramel and banana. Top cakes with caramel-flavoured cream.

8 Using a vegetable peeler, grate chocolate (see page 342); sprinkle over cakes.

lemon meringue cupcakes

Coconut lemon curd cake

125g butter, softened

2 teaspoons finely grated lemon rind

⅔ cup (150g) caster sugar

2 eggs

⅓ cup (80ml) milk

¾ cup (60g) desiccated coconut

1¼ cups (185g) self-raising flour

Lemon curd

4 egg yolks

⅓ cup (75g) caster sugar

2 teaspoons finely grated lemon rind

¼ cup (60ml) lemon juice

40g butter

Coconut meringue

4 egg whites

1 cup (220g) caster sugar

1⅓ cups (95g) shredded coconut, chopped finely

1 Make lemon curd.

2 Preheat oven to 180°C/160°C fan-forced. Line 6-hole texas (¾ cup/180ml) or 12-hole standard (⅓ cup/80ml) muffin pan with paper cases.

3 Beat butter, rind, sugar and eggs in small bowl with electric mixer until light and fluffy.

4 Stir in milk and coconut, then sifted flour. Divide mixture among cases; smooth surface.

5 Bake large cakes about 25 minutes, small cakes about 20 minutes. Turn cakes onto wire rack to cool. Increase oven to 220°C/200°C fan-forced.

6 Cut a 2cm deep hole in the centre of each cake, fill with curd; discard cake tops.

7 Make coconut meringue; spoon into a piping bag fitted with a 1cm plain tube.

8 Pipe meringue on top of each cake (see page 348); place cakes on oven tray.

9 Bake in hot oven 5 minutes or until meringue is browned lightly.

Lemon curd

Combine ingredients in a small heatproof bowl over small saucepan of simmering water, stirring constantly, until mixture thickens slightly and coats the back of a spoon. Remove from heat. Cover tightly; refrigerate curd until cold.

Coconut meringue

Beat egg whites in small bowl with electric mixer until soft peaks form; gradually add sugar, beating until sugar dissolves. Fold in coconut.

sweetheart cupcakes

Raspberry swirl cake
125g butter, softened
½ teaspoon vanilla extract
⅔ cup (150g) caster sugar
2 eggs
1¼ cups (185g) self-raising flour
⅓ cup (80ml) milk
pink food colouring
2 tablespoons raspberry jam
Decorations
½ cup (80g) icing sugar
350g white prepared fondant
⅓ cup (110g) raspberry jam,
   warmed, strained
¼ teaspoon vodka
¼ teaspoon pink petal dust

1 Preheat oven to 180°C/160°C fan-forced. Line 6-hole texas (¾ cup/180ml) or 12-hole standard (⅓ cup/80ml) muffin pan with paper cases.

2 Beat butter, extract, sugar and eggs in small bowl with electric mixer until light and fluffy. Stir in sifted flour and milk, in two batches.

3 Divide mixture evenly between two bowls. Tint one mixture pink; leave other mixture plain. Drop alternate spoonfuls of the two mixtures into cases.

4 Divide jam among cakes, pull a skewer backwards and forwards through mixtures for a swirling effect; smooth surface.

5 Bake large cakes about 30 minutes, small cakes about 20 minutes. Turn cakes onto wire rack to cool.

6 On surface dusted with sifted icing sugar, knead fondant until smooth. Tint fondant with pink colouring; knead into fondant only until marbled (see page 346). Roll out fondant to a thickness of 5mm. Cut out rounds large enough to cover tops of cakes.

7 Blend vodka with petal dust. Using a fine paint brush, paint mixture onto a heart-shaped rubber stamp; press lightly onto fondant rounds. Pinch edges of rounds with fingers.

8 Brush tops of cakes with jam; top with stamped rounds.

chocolate valentine cupcakes

**Double chocolate
raspberry cake**
60g dark eating chocolate,
   chopped coarsely
½ cup (125ml) water
90g butter, softened
1 cup (220g) firmly packed
   brown sugar
2 eggs
⅔ cup (100g) self-raising flour
2 tablespoons cocoa powder
⅓ cup (40g) almond meal
100g frozen raspberries
Decorations
2 tablespoons cocoa powder
900g chocolate prepared
   fondant
⅓ cup (110g) raspberry jam,
   warmed, strained
½ cup (80g) icing sugar
150g red prepared fondant
150g white prepared fondant
pink food colouring

1 Preheat oven to 170°C/150°C
fan-forced. Line 6-hole texas
(¾ cup/180ml) or 12-hole standard
(⅓ cup/80ml) muffin pan with
paper cases.
2 Combine chocolate and the
water in small saucepan; stir over
low heat until smooth.
3 Beat butter, sugar and eggs
in small bowl with electric mixer
until just combined.
4 Stir in sifted flour and cocoa,
almond meal, then warm
chocolate mixture; fold in
raspberries. Divide mixture
among cases; smooth surface.
5 Bake large cakes about
55 minutes, small cakes about
45 minutes. Turn cakes onto
wire rack to cool.
6 Remove cases from cakes.
On a surface dusted with
sifted cocoa, knead chocolate
fondant until smooth. Roll out
to a thickness of 5mm. Cut out
rounds large enough to cover
tops of cakes.

7 Brush cakes with jam; cover
cakes with chocolate fondant.
8 On a surface dusted with
sifted icing sugar, knead white
and red fondant separately until
smooth. Use colouring to tint
100g of the white fondant pink
and remaining white fondant a
paler pink.
9 Roll each coloured fondant
to a thickness of 5mm. Using
heart-shaped cutters of varying
sizes to suit size of cakes, cut
out hearts from fondants using
picture as a guide.
10 Decorate cakes with fondant
hearts, each brushed with a little
water to secure to each other.

coconut cherry heart cupcakes

Choc-chip cherry cake
125g butter, softened
½ teaspoon coconut essence
⅔ cup (150g) caster sugar
2 eggs
⅓ cup (80ml) milk
½ cup (40g) desiccated coconut
⅓ cup (70g) red glacé cherries,
    chopped coarsely
50g dark eating chocolate,
    chopped coarsely
1 cup (150g) self-raising flour
¼ cup (35g) plain flour
Milk chocolate ganache
¼ cup (60ml) cream
100g milk eating chocolate,
    chopped coarsely
Decorations
150g white chocolate Melts,
    melted
pink food colouring

1 Preheat oven to 180°C/160°C fan-forced. Line 6-hole texas (¾ cup/180ml) or 12-hole standard (⅓ cup/80ml) muffin pan with paper cases.
2 Beat butter, essence, sugar and eggs in small bowl with electric mixer until combined.
3 Stir in milk, coconut, cherries and chocolate, then sifted flours. Divide mixture among cases; smooth surface.
4 Bake large cakes about 35 minutes, small cakes about 25 minutes. Turn cakes onto wire rack to cool.
5 Make milk chocolate ganache.
6 Divide white chocolate evenly among three small bowls; tint two portions with two different shades of pink (see page 343).
7 Make three paper piping bags (see page 343); spoon a different coloured chocolate mixture into each bag. Pipe different coloured heart shapes in varying sizes (see page 343), onto baking paper-lined oven tray. Set at room temperature.
8 Spread cakes with ganache; decorate with coloured hearts.

Milk chocolate ganache
Bring cream to a boil in small saucepan; pour over chocolate in small bowl, stir until smooth. Cover bowl; stand at room temperature until ganache is spreadable.

bridal cupcakes

It's important to measure the cake mixture carefully, so the cakes are all the same depth. Make the full amount of mixture; it will be fine standing at room temperature while you bake the 70 cakes in batches. We used standard sized foil cases. You need 64 cakes for the story board. We used scrap booking decorations, available from craft and haberdashery shops and some newsagents.

White chocolate mud cake
500g butter, chopped coarsely
360g white eating chocolate, chopped coarsely
4 cups (880g) caster sugar
2 cups (500ml) milk
3 cups (450g) plain flour
1 cup (150g) self-raising flour
2 teaspoons vanilla extract
4 eggs
Fluffy mock cream frosting
2 tablespoons milk
⅓ cup (80ml) water
1 cup (220g) caster sugar
1 teaspoon gelatine
2 tablespoons water, extra
250g butter, softened
1 teaspoon vanilla extract

Royal icing
1½ cups (240g) pure icing sugar
1 egg white
½ teaspoon lemon juice
Decorations
60cm square cake board
wedding-themed decorations
3m silver ribbon

1 Preheat oven to 170°C/150°C fan-forced. Line two 12-hole standard (⅓ cup/80ml) muffin pans with paper cases.
2 Stir butter, chocolate, sugar and milk in large saucepan, over low heat, until smooth. Transfer to large bowl; cool 15 minutes.
3 Whisk in sifted flours then extract and eggs. Drop exactly 2 level tablespoons of mixture into each case.
4 Bake cakes about 25 minutes. Turn onto wire rack to cool.
5 Meanwhile make fluffy mock cream frosting and royal icing. Cover backs of decorations with baking paper to prevent them from absorbing the frosting.
6 Spread 64 cakes with frosting, place on cake board. Secure ribbon around cakes.

7 Make royal icing; spoon icing into a piping bag fitted with a small plain tube. Pipe hearts onto about 10 of the cakes.
8 Top remaining cakes with wedding-themed decorations.

Fluffy mock cream frosting
Combine milk, the water and sugar in small saucepan, stir over low heat, without boiling, until sugar is dissolved. Sprinkle gelatine over extra water in cup, add to pan; stir syrup until gelatine is dissolved. Cool to room temperature. Beat butter and extract in small bowl with electic mixer, until as white as possible. While motor is operating, gradually pour in cold syrup; beat until light and fluffy. Mixture will thicken on standing.

Royal icing
Sift icing sugar through very fine sieve. Lightly beat egg white in small bowl with electric mixer; add icing sugar, a tablespoon at a time. When icing reaches firm peaks, use a wooden spoon to beat in juice; cover tightly with plastic wrap.

This cake is simply a stack of boxes each containing a cupcake for your wedding guests to take home. The choice of boxes, colours of ribbon and flowers is up to you. Choose the boxes first – size, colour, and quantity. For the ribbon, measure each box, allowing enough ribbon to wrap around and overlap slightly. Our cake has been assembled directly onto a table, but you could also use a covered board. Choose flowers that complement the rest of the wedding flowers. We topped the boxes with a traditional cake for the bride and groom to cut. Alternatively, use a stunning arrangement of flowers. The first recipe explains what we did, using 54 cupcakes. This is only a guide – make the stack larger or smaller, or have more take-home boxes set aside. Most cupcake recipes in this book make 6 texas or 12 standard muffin-sized cakes, you will have to work out the size, type and flavour of cake you'd like, and then work out how many batches of the recipe you'd need.

54 cupcakes
9cm square cake
10cm square cake board
400g white prepared fondant
¼ cup (100g) apricot jam, warmed, strained
400g prepared almond paste
½ cup (80g) icing sugar
20m ribbon
54 x 8cm square gift boxes

1 Bake cupcakes for gift boxes and 9cm square cake of your choice.
2 Secure square cake to board with small piece of fondant made into a paste with water. Brush cake all over with jam.
3 Knead almond paste on surface dusted with sifted icing sugar, cover cake (see page 346); stand overnight.
4 Brush almond paste with jam, cover cake with fondant (see page 346); stand overnight.
5 Secure ribbon to each box with glue or sticky tape.
6 Place one cupcake in each box; stack boxes. Position square cake on top. Decorate with flowers.

These recipes are for the cake on the top tier; use your favourite. All cakes are baked in a greased and lined deep 9cm square pan. A filigree textured plate was used to mark the fondant.

rich fruit cake
60g butter, softened
⅓ cup (75g) firmly packed brown sugar
1 egg
2 teaspoons orange marmalade
375g (2⅓ cups) mixed dried fruit, chopped finely
⅓ (50g) cup plain flour
¼ cup (35g) self-raising flour
½ teaspoon mixed spice
2 tablespoons sweet sherry
2 tablespoons sweet sherry, extra

1 Preheat oven to 150°C/130°C fan-forced.

2 Follow method for Christmas snowflake cupcakes page 113 for cake. Bake cake about 2 hours.

white chocolate mud cake
60g butter, chopped coarsely
40g white chocolate, chopped coarsely
½ cup (110g) caster sugar
¼ cup (60ml) milk
⅓ cup (50g) plain flour
2 tablespoons self-raising flour
½ teaspoon vanilla extract
1 egg, beaten lightly

1 Preheat oven to 170°C/150°C fan-forced.
2 Follow method for Coconut cupcake kisses page 37 for cake.
3 Bake cake about 1 hour.

dark chocolate mud cake
80g butter, chopped coarsely
50g dark chocolate, chopped coarsely
⅔ cup (150g) caster sugar
⅓ cup (80ml) hot water
2 tablespoons coffee liqueur
1 tablespoon instant coffee granules
½ cup (75g) plain flour
1 tablespoon self-raising flour
1 tablespoon cocoa powder
1 egg, beaten lightly

1 Preheat oven to 170°C/150°C fan-forced.
2 Follow method for Florentine cupcakes page 45 for this cake.
3 Bake cake about 1¾ hours.

This recipe makes three individual mini wedding cakes. Arrange the three together at different heights or levels (maybe even interwined with flowers) for a lovely effect.

White chocolate and apricot mud cake

125g butter, chopped coarsely
75g white chocolate, chopped coarsely
1 cup (220g) caster sugar
½ cup (125ml) milk
¾ cup (105g) plain flour
½ cup (75g) self-raising flour
½ cup (75g) finely chopped dried apricots
½ teaspoon vanilla extract
1 egg
⅓ cup (110g) apricot jam, warmed, strained
½ cup (80g) icing sugar
900g white prepared fondant

Modelling fondant

2 teaspoons gelatine
1½ tablespoons water
2 teaspoons glucose syrup
1½ cups (240g) pure icing sugar
½ cup (80g) pure icing sugar, extra

Royal icing

1½ cups (240g) pure icing sugar
1 egg white
½ teaspoon lemon juice

1 Make modelling fondant. On a surface dusted with extra icing sugar, roll fondant to approximately 3mm thick. Cut out flowers using 3.5cm and 1.5cm cutters. Shape flowers using a ball tool (see pages 346); dry on tea towel.
2 Preheat oven to 170°C/150°C fan-forced. Line 6-hole texas (¾ cup/180ml) muffin pan with paper cases.
3 Combine butter, chocolate, sugar and milk in small saucepan; stir over low heat, until smooth. Transfer mixture to medium bowl; cool 15 minutes.
4 Whisk in sifted flours, apricots, then extract and egg; divide mixture among cases.
5 Bake cakes about 45 minutes. Turn cakes onto wire rack to cool.
6 Meanwhile make royal icing. Spoon icing into piping bag fitted with small plain tube, keep icing covered with a damp cloth.
7 Remove cases from cakes. Trim cake edges to make neat cylindrical shapes when stacked. Join two trimmed cakes with apricot jam; brush cakes all over with remaining jam.
8 On surface dusted with sifted icing sugar, knead fondant until smooth. Divide fondant into three equal portions. Roll out each portion to a thickness of 5mm. Cover the three cake stacks individually with fondant. Trim bases and smooth fondant (see page 346).
9 Pipe a little royal icing onto the back of each flower; secure to cake. Pipe some dots in the centre of each flower and around the base of each cake.

Modelling fondant

Sprinkle gelatine over the water in cup; stand cup in small saucepan of simmering water, stirring until gelatine is dissolved; add glucose. Place half the sifted icing sugar in medium bowl, stir in gelatine mixture. Gradually stir in remaining sifted icing sugar. Knead on surface dusted with extra sifted icing sugar until smooth. Wrap tightly in plastic wrap to prevent drying out.

Royal icing

Sift icing sugar through very fine sieve. Lightly beat egg white in small bowl with electric mixer; add icing sugar, a tablespoon at a time. When icing reaches firm peaks, use a wooden spoon to beat in juice; cover tightly with plastic wrap.

lily wedding cakes

Rich fruit cake

90g butter, softened
½ cup (110g) firmly packed
  brown sugar
2 eggs
1 tablespoon orange marmalade
500g (2¾ cups) mixed dried
  fruit, chopped finely
⅔ cup (100g) plain flour
2 tablespoons self-raising flour
1 teaspoon mixed spice
2 tablespoons sweet sherry
2 tablespoons sweet sherry, extra

Modelling fondant
2 teaspoons gelatine
1½ tablespoons water
2 teaspoons glucose syrup
1½ cups (240g) pure icing sugar
½ cup (80g) pure icing sugar, extra

Royal icing
1½ cups (240g) pure icing sugar
1 egg white
½ teaspoon lemon juice

Decorations
⅓ cup (110g) apricot jam,
  warmed, strained
½ cup (80g) icing sugar
900g white prepared fondant
covered 22 gauge wire
florist tape
30 stamens

1 Make modelling fondant. On surface dusted with extra sifted icing sugar, roll a little of the fondant to approximately 2mm thick. Cut out petals using lily petal cutter (see page 347) allowing 6 petals for each cake. Vary size of petals to suit size of cakes. Using frilling tool (see page 347), gently shape petals; attach damp 10cm length wire to each petal (see page 347); allow to dry (see page 347).
2 Preheat oven to 150°C/ 130°C fan-forced. Line 6-hole texas (¾ cup/180ml) or 12-hole standard (⅓ cup/80ml) muffin pan with paper cases.
3 Beat butter, sugar and eggs in small bowl with electric mixer until just combined.
4 Transfer mixture to medium bowl; add marmalade and fruit, mix well.
5 Sift flours and spice over mixture; add sherry, mix well. Divide mixture among cases; smooth surface.
6 Bake large cakes about 1 hour, small cakes about 50 minutes. Remove cakes from oven; brush tops with extra sherry. Cover pan tightly with foil; cool cakes in pan.
7 Meanwhile, assemble lilies using royal icing, stamens and pistles (see page 347).
8 Remove cases from cakes. Brush cakes with jam. On surface dusted with sifted icing sugar, knead prepared fondant until smooth. Divide fondant into six or 12 equal portions. Roll out each portion to a thickness of 5mm. Cover cakes with fondant; trim base and smooth fondant (see page 346).
9 Make royal icing. Spoon royal icing into piping bag fitted with small plain tube. Pipe a continuous line in a cornelli pattern over cakes (see page 348). Secure lilies to cakes.

Modelling fondant
Sprinkle gelatine over the water in cup; stand cup in small saucepan of simmering water, stirring until gelatine is dissolved, add glucose. Sift half the icing sugar in medium bowl, stir in gelatine mixture. Gradually stir in remaining sifted icing sugar, knead on surface dusted with extra sifted icing sugar until smooth. Wrap tightly in plastic wrap to prevent drying out.

Royal icing
Sift icing sugar through very fine sieve. Lightly beat egg white in small bowl; add icing sugar, a tablespoon at a time, beating well after each addition. When icing reaches firm peaks, add juice; beat well. Cover tightly with plastic wrap.

lace wedding cakes

If your oven won't hold three sets of muffin pans, it's fine to leave the mixture standing at room temperature while the first batch bakes. We used three cake stands stacked on top of each other to display the cakes. They measured 17cm, 24cm and 34cm in diameter. We used a plastic filigree textured plate to mark the icing, available from craft or haberdashery shops. Mix and match the colours of the plates, cakes and flowers to suit the occasion.

Rich fruit cake
250g butter, softened
1¼ cups (250g) firmly packed
   brown sugar
4 eggs
2 tablespoons orange
   marmalade
1.5kg (7¾ cups) mixed dried
   fruit, chopped finely
1½ cups (225g) plain flour
½ cup (75g) self-raising flour
2 teaspoons mixed spice
½ cup (125ml) sweet sherry
¼ cup (30g) blanched whole
   almonds
2 tablespoons sweet sherry, extra
Decorations
½ cup (80g) icing sugar
750g white prepared fondant
filigree textured plate
½ cup (160g) orange marmalade,
   warmed, strained
silver lustre

1 Preheat oven to 150°C/ 130°C fan-forced. Line three 12-hole standard (⅓ cup/80ml) muffin pans with silver foil and paper cases.
2 Beat butter, sugar and eggs in small bowl with electric mixer until just combined.
3 Transfer mixture to large bowl, add marmalade and fruit; mix well.
4 Sift flours and spice over mixture, add sherry; mix well.
5 Place 2 level tablespoons of mixture into each case; smooth surface.
6 Bake cakes about 50 minutes. Remove cakes from oven; brush tops with extra sherry. Cover pan tightly with foil; cool cakes in pan.
7 On surface dusted with sifted icing sugar, knead fondant until smooth. Roll out to a thickness of 5mm. Using a 7cm round fluted cutter cut out 36 rounds.
8 Using a filigree textured plate, gently press an imprint onto each fondant round (see page 351).
9 Brush cakes with marmalade; top with fondant rounds. Carefully brush silver lustre over pattern on fondant.

deluxe chocolate wedding cakes

You need to buy triple the quantity of the ingredients for the cake recipe below. You will need to make three separate batches, do not double or triple this recipe. It's important to measure the cake mixture carefully so the cakes are all the same depth. The mixture will be fine standing at room temperature while you bake the cakes in batches. Each batch will make 40 cakes. You need 120 standard muffin paper cases.

Mocha mud cake
500g butter, chopped coarsely
300g dark eating chocolate, chopped coarsely
4 cups (880g) caster sugar
2 cups (500ml) water
⅔ cup (160ml) coffee liqueur
2 tablespoons instant coffee granules
3 cups (450g) plain flour
½ cup (75g) self-raising flour
½ cup (50g) cocoa powder
4 eggs

Dark chocolate ganache
600ml thickened cream
800g dark eating chocolate, chopped coarsely

Decorations
15cm, 20cm, 30cm, 35cm and 45cm round boards
5m x 1.5cm cotton lace ribbon
4 empty cans, 9cm tall and 5cm in diameter
wrapping paper, for cans
200g milk eating chocolate
½ cup (115g) finely chopped glacé ginger
½ cup (10g) dried rose petals
¼ cup (25g) roasted coffee beans
2 miniature brandy snaps

1 Preheat oven to 170°C/150°C fan-forced. Line two 12-hole standard (⅓ cup/80ml) muffin pans with paper cases.
2 Combine butter, chocolate, sugar, the water, liqueur and coffee in large saucepan; stir over low heat until smooth. Transfer mixture to large bowl; cool 15 minutes.
3 Whisk in sifted flours and cocoa, then eggs. Pour exactly ¼ cup of mixture into each case.
4 Bake cakes about 40 minutes. Turn cakes onto wire racks to cool.
5 Make dark chocolate ganache.
6 Attach ribbon to edge of round boards, using double sided tape. Cover cans with wrapping paper. Glue cans to centre of the four largest boards. Stack boards from the bottom tier up, as shown in picture.
7 Spread all cakes with ganache. Decorate cakes as shown with chocolate curls using vegetable peeler (see page 342), glacé ginger, coffee beans, rose petals and brandy snaps.
8 Place cakes on boards.

Dark chocolate ganache
Bring cream to a boil in medium saucepan, pour over chocolate in large bowl; stir until smooth. Cover bowl; refrigerate, about 30 minutes or until ganache is of a spreadable consistency.

Almond buttercake

150g butter, softened
½ teaspoon almond essence
⅔ cup (150g) caster sugar
2 eggs
⅓ cup (50g) self-raising flour
½ cup (75g) plain flour
½ cup (60g) almond meal

Choux pastry

60g butter
¾ cup (180ml) water
¾ cup (105g) plain flour
3 eggs, beaten lightly

Vanilla custard

1¼ cups (310ml) milk
1 vanilla bean, split
4 egg yolks
½ cup (110g) caster sugar
¼ cup (40g) cornflour

Toffee

1 cup (220g) caster sugar
½ cup (125ml) water

1 Make choux pastry; make vanilla custard.
2 Preheat oven to 180°C/160°C fan-forced. Line 6-hole texas (¾ cup/180ml) or 12-hole standard (⅓ cup/80ml) muffin pan with paper cases.
3 Beat butter, essence, sugar and eggs in small bowl with electric mixer until light and fluffy.
4 Stir in sifted flours and almond meal, in two batches. Divide mixture among cases; smooth surface.
5 Bake large cakes about 30 minutes, small cakes about 20 minutes. Turn cakes onto wire rack to cool.
6 Cut a 2cm deep hole in the centre of each cake, fill with custard; replace lid.
7 Spread tops of cakes with a little more custard. Top with a layer of puffs. Stack remaining puffs on cakes dipping each in a little custard.
8 Make toffee; drizzle over puffs.

Choux pastry

Preheat oven to 220°C/200°C fan-forced. Grease oven trays, line with baking paper. Combine butter with the water in medium saucepan; bring to a boil. Add flour; beat with wooden spoon over heat until mixture forms a smooth ball. Transfer mixture to small bowl; beat in egg with electric mixer in about six batches until mixture becomes glossy. Spoon mixture into piping bag fitted with 1cm plain tube. Pipe about 300 tiny dollops of pastry (about ¼ level teaspoon) 2cm apart, onto trays (see page 348); bake 7 minutes. Reduce oven to 180°C/160°C fan-forced; bake for further 5 minutes or until puffs are crisp. Repeat with remaining mixture.

Vanilla custard

Bring milk and vanilla bean to a boil in small saucepan; discard vanilla bean. Meanwhile, beat egg yolks, sugar and cornflour in small bowl with electric mixer until thick. With motor operating, gradually beat in warm milk. Return custard to same pan; stir over heat until mixture boils and thickens. Cover surface of custard with plastic wrap; cool.

Toffee

Combine sugar with the water in small heavy-based saucepan. Stir over heat, without boiling, until sugar dissolves; bring to a boil. Reduce heat; simmer, uncovered, without stirring, until mixture is golden brown. Remove from heat; stand until bubbles subside before using.

toffee tumble
cupcakes

apple custard tea cakes

Apple custard tea cakes
90g butter
½ teaspoon vanilla extract
½ cup (110g) caster sugar
2 eggs
¾ cup (110g) self-raising flour
¼ cup (30g) custard powder
2 tablespoons milk
1 large (200g) unpeeled apple,
    cored, sliced finely
30g butter, extra, melted
1 tablespoon caster sugar, extra
½ teaspoon ground cinnamon
Custard
1 tablespoon custard powder
1 tablespoon caster sugar
½ cup (125ml) milk
¼ teaspoon vanilla extract

1 Make custard.
2 Preheat oven to 180°C/160°C fan-forced. Line 6-hole texas (¾ cup/180ml) or 12-hole standard (⅓ cup/80ml) muffin pan with paper cases.
3 Beat butter, extract, sugar, eggs, flour, custard powder and milk in small bowl with electric mixer on low speed until ingredients are just combined. Increase speed to medium, beat until mixture is changed to a paler colour.
4 Divide half the mixture among cases. Top with custard, then remaining cake mixture; spread mixture to cover custard. Top with apple slices, pressing slightly into cake.
5 Bake large cakes about 40 minutes, small cakes about 30 minutes.
6 Brush hot cakes with extra butter, then sprinkle with combined extra sugar and cinnamon. Turn cakes onto wire rack. Serve warm or cold.

Custard
Blend custard powder and sugar with milk and extract in small saucepan; stir over heat until mixture boils and thickens. Remove from heat; cover surface with plastic wrap. Cool.

flower cupcakes

Banana sour cream cake
90g butter, softened
½ cup (110g) firmly packed
    brown sugar
2 eggs
½ cup (75g) self-raising flour
½ cup (75g) plain flour
½ teaspoon bicarbonate of soda
½ teaspoon mixed spice
⅔ cup (200g) mashed overripe
    banana
⅓ cup (80g) sour cream
2 tablespoons milk
Modelling fondant
2 teaspoons gelatine
1½ tablespoons water
2 teaspoons glucose syrup
1½ cups (240g) pure icing sugar
½ cup (80g) pure icing sugar, extra
Cream cheese frosting
30g butter, softened
80g cream cheese, softened
1½ cups (240g) icing sugar
blue food colouring
Decorations
½ cup (80g) icing sugar
400g white prepared fondant
pink and yellow food colouring
pink petal dust

1 Make modelling fondant.
On a surface dusted with extra
sifted icing sugar, roll modelling
fondant to approximately 3mm
thick. Cut out butterfly wings
using butterfly cutter and shape
butterfly bodies (see page 346);
allow to dry.
2 Preheat oven to 180°C/160°C
fan-forced. Line 6-hole texas
(¾ cup/180ml) or 12-hole standard
(⅓ cup/80ml) muffin pan with
paper cases.
3 Beat butter, sugar and eggs
in small bowl with electric mixer
until light and fluffy.
4 Stir in sifted dry ingredients,
then banana, cream and milk.
Divide mixture among cases;
smooth surface.
5 Bake large cakes about
35 minutes, small cakes about
25 minutes. Turn cakes onto
wire rack to cool.
6 Make cream cheese frosting.
Assemble butterflies (see pages
346 and 347).
7 On surface dusted with sifted
icing sugar, knead prepared
fondant until smooth. Using
colouring, tint three-quarters
of the fondant pink and one-
quarter yellow. Roll out pink

fondant to a thickness of 5mm;
cut out petal shapes to suit the
size of the cakes. Shape yellow
fondant into balls; gently flatten
until large enough to form centre
of flowers.
8 Spread cakes with frosting.
Decorate with petals and
centres. Position a butterfly on
each cake; dust wings with pink
petal dust.

Modelling fondant
Sprinkle gelatine over the
water in cup; stand cup in small
saucepan of simmering water,
stirring until gelatine is dissolved,
add glucose. Sift half the icing
sugar into medium bowl; stir in
gelatine mixture. Gradually stir
in remaining sifted icing sugar,
knead on surface dusted with
extra sifted icing sugar until
smooth. Wrap tightly in plastic
wrap to prevent drying out.

Cream cheese frosting
Beat butter and cheese in small
bowl with electric mixer until light
and fluffy; gradually beat in sfited
icing sugar. Tint with colouring.

100g dark chocolate Melts,
  melted
⅓ cup (110g) chocolate
  hazelnut spread
¼ cup (25g) hazelnut meal
1 tablespoon finely crushed ice
  cream wafer or cone
12 hazelnuts, toasted
1 tablespoon hazelnut meal,
  extra

1 Using small, clean paint brush, paint chocolate thickly inside 12 x 2.5cm foil cases (see page 342). Place cases on tray; refrigerate about 5 minutes or until chocolate sets. Peel away cases (see pages 343).
2 Combine spread and hazelnut meal in small bowl; spoon mixture into piping bag fitted with 1.5cm fluted tube.
3 Divide pieces of wafer and hazelnuts among cases. Pipe chocolate mixture into cases. Sprinkle with a little extra hazelnut meal.

chocolate hazelnut cups

citrus cupcakes

We used green, orange and yellow paper muffin cases to match the decorations of these lovely cakes.

Poppy seed citrus cake
¼ cup (40g) poppy seeds
2 tablespoons milk
125g butter, softened
1 teaspoon finely grated lemon rind
1 teaspoon finely grated lime rind
⅔ cup (150g) caster sugar
2 eggs
1 cup (150g) self-raising flour
⅓ cup (50g) plain flour
⅓ cup (40g) almond meal
¼ cup (60ml) orange juice
Decorations
½ cup (80g) icing sugar
450g white prepared fondant
green, orange and yellow food colouring
⅓ cup (110g) orange marmalade, warmed, strained
2 tablespoons green sprinkles
2 tablespoons orange sprinkles
2 tablespoons yellow sprinkles

1 Preheat oven to 180°C/160°C fan-forced. Line 6-hole texas (¾ cup/180ml) or 12-hole standard (⅓ cup/80ml) muffin pan with paper cases.
2 Combine seeds and milk in small bowl; stand 20 minutes.
3 Beat butter, rinds, sugar and eggs in small bowl with electric mixer until light and fluffy.
4 Stir in sifted flours, almond meal, juice and poppy seed mixture. Divide mixture among cases; smooth surface.
5 Bake large cakes about 30 minutes, small cakes about 20 minutes. Turn cakes onto wire rack to cool.
6 On surface dusted with sifted icing sugar, knead fondant until smooth. Reserve 100g of fondant; enclose in plastic wrap. Divide remaining fondant into three equal portions; tint green, orange and yellow by kneading in colouring (see page 346). Wrap separately in plastic wrap.

7 Roll each of the coloured portions to a thickness of 5mm. Cut out rounds large enough to cover tops of cakes. Brush tops of cakes with marmalade, position rounds on cakes.
8 Roll reserved fondant into very thin lengths, cut off small pieces to represent seeds. Position lengths on top of cakes, using a little water, to represent segments.
9 Fill segments with matching coloured sprinkles; position fondant seeds.

sweet violet cupcakes

Lemon cream cheese cake
90g butter, softened
90g cream cheese, softened
2 teaspoons finely grated
  lemon rind
⅔ cup (150g) caster sugar
2 eggs
⅓ cup (50g) self-raising flour
½ cup (75g) plain flour
Lemon cream cheese frosting
30g butter, softened
80g cream cheese, softened
1 teaspoon finely grated
  lemon rind
1½ cups (240g) icing sugar
Decorations
tea-lights
fresh violets

1 Preheat oven to 180°C/160°C fan-forced. Line 6-hole texas (¾ cup/180ml) or 12-hole standard (⅓ cup/80ml) muffin pan with paper cases.
2 Beat butter, cheese, rind, sugar and eggs in small bowl with electric mixer until light and fluffy.
3 Add sifted flours; beat on low speed until just combined. Divide mixture among cases; smooth surface.
4 Bake large cakes about 35 minutes, small cakes about 25 minutes. Turn cakes onto wire rack to cool.
5 Make lemon cream cheese frosting. Spread cakes with frosting; decorate with tea-lights and violets.

Lemon cream cheese frosting
Beat butter, cream cheese and rind in small bowl with electric mixer until light and fluffy; gradually beat in sifted icing sugar.

black forest cupcakes

Cherry chocolate mud cake
425g can pitted cherries in syrup
165g butter, chopped coarsely
100g dark eating chocolate,
    chopped coarsely
1⅓ cups (295g) caster sugar
¼ cup (60ml) cherry brandy
1 cup (150g) plain flour
2 tablespoons self-raising flour
2 tablespoons cocoa powder
1 egg
Decorations
⅔ cup (160ml) thickened cream,
    whipped
2 teaspoons cherry brandy
100g dark eating chocolate

1 Preheat oven to 170°C/150°C fan-forced. Line 6-hole texas (¾ cup/180ml) or 12-hole standard (⅓ cup/80ml) muffin pan with paper cases.

2 Drain cherries; reserve syrup. Process ½ cup (110g) cherries with ½ cup (125ml) of the syrup until smooth. Halve remaining cherries; reserve for decorating cakes. Discard remaining syrup.

3 Combine butter, chocolate, sugar, brandy and cherry puree in small saucepan; stir over low heat until chocolate is melted. Transfer mixture to medium bowl; cool 15 minutes.

4 Whisk in sifted flours and cocoa, then egg. Divide mixture among cases; smooth surface.

5 Bake large cakes about 55 minutes, small cakes about 45 minutes. Turn cakes onto wire rack to cool.

6 Top cakes with remaining cherry halves and combined cream and cherry brandy. Using a vegetable peeler, make small chocolate curls (see page 342); sprinkle over cakes.

passionfruit curd cupcakes

Passionfruit buttercake
90g butter, softened
½ cup (110g) caster sugar
2 eggs
1 cup (150g) self-raising flour
¼ cup (60ml) passionfruit pulp
Passionfruit curd
2 eggs, beaten lightly
⅓ cup caster sugar
1 tablespoon lemon juice
¼ cup passionfruit pulp
60g butter, chopped coarsely
Decorations
85g packet passionfruit jelly
1 cup (250ml) boiling water
1 cup (80g) desiccated coconut
½ cup (125ml) thickened cream,
  whipped

1 Make passionfruit curd.
2 Preheat oven to 180°C/160°C fan-forced. Line 6-hole texas (¾ cup/180ml) or 12-hole standard (⅓ cup/80ml) muffin pan with paper cases.
3 Beat butter, sugar, eggs and flour in small bowl with electric mixer on low speed until ingredients are just combined. Increase speed to medium, beat until mixture is changed to a paler colour. Stir in passionfruit pulp.
4 Divide mixture among cases; smooth surface.
5 Bake large cakes about 25 minutes, small cakes about 20 minutes. Turn cakes onto wire rack to cool.
6 Dissolve jelly in the water. Refrigerate about 30 minutes or until set to the consistency of unbeaten egg white.
7 Remove cases from cakes. Roll cakes in jelly; leave cakes to stand in jelly for 15 minutes turning occasionally. Roll cakes in coconut; place on wire rack over tray. Refrigerate 30 minutes.
8 Cut cakes in half; fill with curd and cream.

Passionfruit curd
Combine ingredients in a small heatproof bowl, place over a small saucepan of simmering water; stir constantly until mixture thickens slightly and coats the back of a spoon. Remove from heat. Cover tightly; refrigerate curd until cold.

orange cupcake bouquet

Orange almond cake
6 slices (120g) glacé orange
75g butter, softened
1 teaspoon finely grated
    orange rind
⅓ cup (75g) caster sugar
1 egg
2 tablespoons self-raising flour
¼ cup (35g) plain flour
¼ cup (30g) almond meal

Decorations
15cm polystyrene craft ball
24 double-ended wooden
    toothpicks
2 sheets tissue paper
ribbon
fresh flowers
florist tape

1 Cut each orange slice into 20 tiny wedges.

2 Preheat oven to 180°C/160°C fan-forced. Line two 12-hole mini (1 tablespoon/20ml) muffin pans with paper cases.

3 Beat butter, rind, sugar and egg in small bowl with electric mixer until light and fluffy.

4 Stir in sifted flours and almond meal. Divide mixture among cases; smooth surface. Top each cake with five orange wedges.

5 Bake cakes about 15 minutes. Turn cakes onto wire rack to cool.

6 Using a serrated knife cut about quarter of the ball away, so the ball will sit flat. Using toothpicks, secure cakes to ball. Place bouquet on a small stand; wrap with paper and ribbon. Bind ends of fresh flowers with florist tape; position flowers between cakes.

5 x 60g Mars bars
50g butter
3½ cups (120g) Rice Bubbles
200g milk eating chocolate,
   melted

1 Line a 12-hole standard
(⅓ cup/80ml) muffin pan with
paper cases.
2 Chop four of the Mars bars
coarsely; cut remaining bar
into slices.
3 Place chopped Mars bars in
medium saucepan with butter;
stir over low heat until smooth.
Stir in Rice Bubbles.
4 Press mixture into cases,
spread with chocolate; top with
sliced Mars bar. Refrigerate
about 30 minutes or until set.

no-bake chocolate cakes

pineapple hibiscus cupcakes

Pineapple carrot cake
½ cup (125ml) vegetable oil
3 eggs, beaten lightly
1½ cups (225g) self-raising flour
¾ cup (165g) caster sugar
½ teaspoon ground cinnamon
2 cups (440g) firmly packed
   coarsely grated carrot
¾ cup (160g) drained crushed
   pineapple

Pineapple flowers
1 tablespoon caster sugar
1 tablespoon water
12 wafer thin slices fresh
   pineapple

Lemon cream cheese frosting
30g butter, softened
80g cream cheese, softened
1 teaspoon finely grated
   lemon rind
1½ cups (240g) icing sugar

1 Make pineapple flowers.
2 Preheat oven to 180°C/160°C
fan-forced. Line a 6-hole texas
(¾ cup/180ml) or 12-hole standard
(⅓ cup/80ml) muffin pan with
paper cases.
3 Combine oil, eggs, flour, sugar
and cinnamon in medium bowl;
stir until combined. Stir in carrot
and pineapple.
4 Divide mixture among cases.
5 Bake large cakes about
40 minutes, small cakes about
30 minutes. Turn cakes onto
wire rack to cool.
6 Make lemon cream cheese
frosting; spread on top of cakes.
Decorate with pineapple flowers.

Pineapple flowers
Preheat oven to 120°C/100°C
fan-forced. Stir sugar and
the water together in a small
saucepan over low heat until
sugar has dissolved; boil 1 minute.
Brush both sides of pineapple
slices with sugar syrup. Place
slices in a single layer on wire
racks over oven trays (see page
351). Dry pineapple in oven for
about 1 hour. Immediately remove
slices from rack; carefully shape
into flowers. Dry over an upturned
egg carton (see page 351).

Lemon cream cheese frosting
Beat butter, cream cheese and
rind in small bowl with electric
mixer until light and fluffy;
gradually beat in sifted icing sugar.

chocolate ginger gum nut cupcakes

Chocolate ginger mud cake
165g butter, chopped coarsely
100g dark eating chocolate,
  chopped coarsely
1⅓ cups (295g) caster sugar
⅔ cup (160ml) green ginger wine
¼ cup (60ml) water
1 cup (150g) plain flour
2 tablespoons self-raising flour
2 tablespoons cocoa powder
1 egg
⅓ cup (75g) finely chopped
  glacé ginger
Chocolate decorations
100g dark chocolate Melts,
  melted
100g milk chocolate Melts,
  melted
fresh rose leaves, washed
Dark chocolate ganache
½ cup (125ml) thickened cream
200g dark eating chocolate,
  chopped coarsely

1 Make chocolate decorations
– gum nuts, branches and leaves.
2 Preheat oven to 170°C/150°C
fan-forced. Line 6-hole texas
(¾ cup/180ml) or 12-hole standard
(⅓ cup/80ml) muffin pan with
paper cases.
3 Combine butter, chocolate,
sugar, wine and the water in
small saucepan; stir over low
heat until smooth. Transfer to
medium bowl; cool 15 minutes.
4 Whisk in sifted flours and
cocoa, then egg. Stir in ginger.
Divide mixture among cases.
5 Bake large cakes about 1 hour,
small cakes about 50 minutes.
Turn cakes onto wire rack to cool.
6 Make dark chocolate ganache.
7 Pour ganache over cakes; set
at room temperature.
8 Decorate cakes with chocolate
gum nuts, branches and leaves.

Chocolate decorations
For gum nuts, spread dark
chocolate onto a cold surface;
when set, pull a melon baller over
chocolate to make gum nuts (see
page 342). For branches, spoon
half the milk chocolate into paper
piping bag (see page 343); pipe
branches onto a baking-paper-
lined tray (see page 343); leave to
set. Gently lift branches off paper.
For leaves, using a small, clean
paint brush, paint remaining milk
chocolate thickly on one side of
each leaf (see page 342), place
on baking paper-lined tray; leave
to set. Carefully peel away and
discard leaves (see page 343).

Dark chocolate ganache
Bring cream to a boil in small
saucepan; pour over chocolate
in small bowl; stir until smooth.
Stand at room temperature
until ganache is a thick pouring
consistency.

easter egg cupcake baskets

Light fruit cake

125g butter, softened

½ teaspoon almond essence

⅔ cup (150g) caster sugar

2 eggs

⅔ cup (140g) red and green
   glacé cherries, quartered

⅓ cup (55g) sultanas

½ cup (70g) slivered almonds

⅔ cup (100g) plain flour

⅓ cup (50g) self-raising flour

¼ cup (60ml) milk

Royal icing

3 cups (480g) pure icing sugar

2 egg whites

1 teaspoon lemon juice

brown food colouring

Decorations

300g sugared almonds or
   mini chocolate eggs

1 Preheat oven to 170°C/150°C fan-forced. Line 6-hole texas (¾ cup/180ml) or 12-hole standard (⅓ cup/80ml) muffin pan with paper cases.

2 Beat butter, essence, sugar and eggs in small bowl with electric mixer until light and fluffy.

3 Add fruit and nuts; mix well. Stir in sifted flours and milk. Divide mixture among cases; smooth surface.

4 Bake large cakes about 45 minutes, small cakes about 40 minutes. Turn cakes onto wire rack to cool.

5 Make royal icing.

6 Remove cases from cakes. Pipe basket weave around cakes (see page 349); leave to dry for 3 hours or overnight.

7 Fill baskets with sugared almonds or chocolate eggs.

Royal icing

Sift icing sugar through very fine sieve. Lightly beat egg whites in small bowl with electric mixer; beat in icing sugar, a tablespoon at a time. When icing reaches firm peaks, use wooden spoon to beat in juice and colouring; cover tightly with plastic wrap.

spicy christmas cupcakes

Make these festive cupcakes for Christmas; serve warm with brandy butter, whipped cream or custard.

Buttermilk spice cake
½ cup (110g) firmly packed
    brown sugar
½ cup (75g) plain flour
½ cup (75g) self-raising flour
¼ teaspoon bicarbonate of soda
1 teaspoon ground ginger
½ teaspoon ground cinnamon
¼ teaspoon ground nutmeg
90g butter, softened
1 egg
¼ cup (60ml) buttermilk
2 tablespoons golden syrup
Christmas decorations
½ cup (80g) icing sugar
100g white prepared fondant
5cm lengths of covered
    24 gauge wire
Filling
½ cup (180g) fruit mince
1 tablespoon icing sugar

1 Make Christmas decorations.
2 Preheat oven to 180°C/160°C fan-forced. Line 6-hole texas (¾ cup/180ml) or 12-hole standard (⅓ cup/80ml) muffin pan with paper cases.
3 Sift dry ingredients into small bowl, add remaining ingredients; beat with electric mixer on low speed until ingredients are combined. Increase speed to medium, beat until mixture is smooth and changed to a paler colour. Divide mixture among cases; smooth surface.
4 Bake large cakes about 35 minutes, small cakes about 25 minutes. Turn cakes onto wire rack to cool for 5 minutes.
5 Cut a 2cm deep hole in the centre of each warm cake; discard cake rounds. Fill centres with fruit mince mixture. Top with wired fondant shapes; dust with a little sifted icing sugar.

Christmas decorations
On surface dusted with sifted icing sugar, knead fondant until smooth. Roll out to 1cm thickness. Cut out fondant shapes using Christmas cutters. Insert a length of damp wire into each shape. Dry overnight on baking-paper-lined tray.

Filling
Warm fruit mince in small saucepan over low heat; stir in icing sugar. Or, heat fruit mince in a microwave oven for about 30 seconds on HIGH (100%); stir in icing sugar.

christmas tree cupcakes

Edible glitter is a non-metallic decoration available at cake decorating shops.

Tropical fruit cake
125g butter, softened
1 teaspoon coconut essence
²⁄₃ cup (150g) caster sugar
2 eggs
1 cup (180g) finely chopped
   dried tropical fruit salad
½ cup (75g) macadamia nuts,
   chopped coarsely
²⁄₃ cup (100g) plain flour
⅓ cup (50g) self-raising flour
⅓ cup (25g) desiccated coconut
¼ cup (60ml) milk
Coconut ice frosting
2 egg whites
1 teaspoon coconut essence
1½ cups (240g) icing sugar
1 cup (90g) desiccated coconut
Decorations
10 star fruit, approximately
green edible glitter

1 Preheat oven to 170°C/150°C fan forced. Line 6-hole texas (¾ cup/180ml) or 12-hole standard (⅓ cup/80ml) muffin pan with paper cases.
2 Beat butter, essence, sugar and eggs in small bowl with electric mixer until light and fluffy.
3 Stir in dried fruit and nuts, then sifted flours, coconut and milk. Divide mixture among cases; smooth surface.
4 Bake large cakes about 45 minutes, small cakes about 35 minutes. Turn cakes onto wire racks to cool.
5 Make coconut ice frosting; top cakes with frosting.
6 Cut star fruit into 5mm slices. Arrange slices to make Christmas tree shapes of varying heights and sizes depending on size of cakes used. Use toothpicks or trimmed bamboo skewers to hold star fruit in position. Sprinkle with glitter.

Coconut ice frosting
Beat egg whites and essence in small bowl with electric mixer until foamy. Beat in sifted icing sugar in about four batches; stir in coconut.

Lustre is a powder available from cake decorating shops and craft shops in metallic shades, and is applied with a paintbrush.

Rich fruit cake

90g butter, softened
½ cup (110g) firmly packed
   brown sugar
2 eggs
1 tablespoon orange marmalade
500g (2¾ cups) mixed dried fruit,
   chopped finely
⅔ cup (100g) plain flour
2 tablespoons self-raising flour
1 teaspoon mixed spice
2 tablespoons sweet sherry
2 tablespoons sweet sherry, extra

Decorations

½ cup (80g) icing sugar
300g white prepared fondant
½ teaspoon silver lustre
½ teaspoon vodka
silver cachous
⅓ cup (110g) apricot jam,
   warmed, strained

1 Preheat oven to 150°C/130°C fan-forced. Line 6-hole texas (¾ cup/180ml) or 12-hole standard (⅓ cup/80ml) muffin pan with paper cases.
2 Beat butter, sugar and eggs in small bowl with electric mixer until just combined.
3 Stir in marmalade and fruit; mix well.
4 Sift flours and spice over mixture; add sherry, mix well. Divide mixture among cases; smooth surface.
5 Bake large cakes about 1 hour, small cakes about 50 minutes. Remove cakes from oven; brush tops with extra sherry. Cover pan tightly with foil; cool cakes in pan.

6 On surface dusted with sifted icing sugar, knead fondant until smooth; roll out to a thickness of 5mm. Using a fluted cutter, cut out rounds large enough to almost cover tops of cakes.
7 Using a cardboard snowflake template, gently press an imprint into the centre of each fondant round (see page 351).
8 Brush cakes with jam; top with fondant rounds. Blend lustre with vodka, paint onto snowflakes; push silver cachous gently into rounds.

christmas snowflake cupcakes

jewel cupcakes

Festive jewel cake

2 rings (55g) glacé pineapple
3 whole (85g) glacé apricots
1 cup (140g) seeded dried dates
⅔ cup (140g) red and green
  glacé cherries
½ cup (80g) whole blanched
  almonds
1 cup (160g) brazil nuts
2 eggs
⅓ cup (75g) firmly packed
  brown sugar
1 tablespoon dark rum
60g butter, softened
¼ cup (35g) plain flour
2 tablespoons self-raising flour

Topping

3 rings (80g) glacé pineapple
½ cup (100g) red and green
  glacé cherries, halved
½ cup (80g) brazil nuts
½ cup (80g) whole blanched
  almonds
⅓ cup (110g) apricot jam,
  warmed, strained

1 Preheat oven to 150°C/130°C fan-forced. Line 6-hole texas (¾ cup/180ml) or 12-hole standard (⅓ cup/80ml) muffin pan with paper cases.
2 Coarsely chop pineapple and apricots, halve cherries and nuts for large cakes. Chop fruit and nuts slightly smaller for small cakes.
3 Combine fruit and nuts in medium bowl.
4 Beat eggs in small bowl with electric mixer until thick and creamy; add sugar, rum and butter, beat until just combined.
5 Stir egg mixture into fruit mixture with sifted flours. Divide mixture among cases; press firmly into cases.
6 Make topping; divide evenly over cakes.
7 Bake large cakes about 1¼ hours, small cakes about 1 hour; cover cakes loosely with foil halfway through baking time. Cool cakes in pan.
8 Remove cakes from pan; brush tops with jam.

Topping
Coarsely chop pineapple; combine with remaining fruit and nuts for large cakes. Chop fruit and nuts slightly smaller for small cakes. Combine fruit and nuts in small bowl; mix well.

cheesecakes

Here's a simple recipe for sweet success: whether you choose classic or less predictable flavours and ingredients, it's never a mistake to serve cheesecake. Everything that makes them delicious – their rich, creamy density, their sweet, saucy toppings, their unexpectedly delicious bases – are all bliss to the senses. And, as if that isn't enough, they can be made ahead. With their sophisticated tastes and simple preparation, these versatile recipes solve the never-ending dilemma of what to serve for dessert.

baked cheesecakes

Originating in lavish patisseries and coffee houses in Europe, the timeless elegance of the simple baked cheesecake has since been claimed by sweet-tooths the world over.

lemon curd cheesecake

250g plain sweet biscuits
125g butter, melted
Filling
750g cream cheese, softened
2 teaspoons finely grated
   lemon rind
½ cup (110g) caster sugar
3 eggs
Lemon curd
45g butter
½ cup (110g) caster sugar
1 egg, beaten lightly, strained
1 teaspoon finely grated
   lemon rind
2 tablespoons lemon juice

1 Process biscuits until fine. Add butter, process until combined. Press mixture over base and side of 22cm springform tin. Place tin on oven tray; refrigerate 30 minutes.
2 Preheat oven to 160°C/140°C fan-forced.
3 Make filling by beating cheese, rind and sugar in medium bowl with electric mixer until smooth; beat in eggs, one at a time.
4 Pour filling into tin; bake about 1 hour. Cool cheesecake in oven with door ajar.
5 Make lemon curd.
6 Spread cheesecake with lemon curd; refrigerate 3 hours or overnight.

Lemon curd
Combine ingredients in small heatproof bowl. Place bowl over small saucepan of simmering water (water must not touch bottom of bowl); cook, stirring constantly, about 20 minutes or until mixture coats the back of a spoon. Remove bowl from saucepan immediately; cover curd with plastic wrap, cool to room temperature.

Serves 10

lemon meringue cheesecakes

1½ cups (225g) plain flour
¼ cup (40g) icing sugar
125g cold butter, chopped
2 egg yolks
1 tablespoon iced water
Filling
375g cream cheese, softened
1 tablespoon finely grated
   lemon rind
1 egg
1 egg yolk
1 tablespoon lemon juice
1 tablespoon plain flour
½ cup (180g) lemon-flavoured
   spread
Meringue
2 egg whites
½ cup (110g) caster sugar
½ teaspoon cornflour

1 Grease six deep 10cm fluted loose-based flan tins.
2 Process flour, sugar and butter until crumbly. Add egg yolks and the water, pulse until ingredients come together. Knead pastry on floured surface until smooth. Wrap in plastic; refrigerate 30 minutes.
3 Divide pastry into six portions; roll each between sheets of baking paper until large enough to line tins. Ease dough into tins, press into sides; trim edges. Refrigerate 30 minutes.
4 Preheat oven to 200°C/180°C fan-forced.
5 Cover pastry cases with baking paper, fill with dried beans or rice; place on oven tray. Bake 10 minutes. Remove paper and beans; bake about 10 minutes or until pastry is browned lightly. Cool.
6 Reduce oven temperature to 160°C/140°C fan-forced.

7 Make filling by beating cheese, rind, egg and egg yolk in small bowl with electric mixer until smooth. Beat in juice, flour and lemon spread.
8 Divide filling among pastry cases. Bake about 25 minutes; cool in oven with door ajar. Refrigerate 3 hours or overnight.
9 Preheat oven to 240°C/220°C fan-forced.
10 Make meringue.
11 Place cheesecakes on oven tray. Rough surface of cheesecakes with fork; pipe or spoon meringue over filling. Bake about 3 minutes or until browned lightly. Cool 10 minutes before serving.

Meringue
Beat egg whites in small bowl with electric mixer until soft peaks form; gradually add sugar, beating until sugar dissolves between additions. Fold in cornflour.

Makes 6

sour cream cheesecake

250g plain sweet biscuits
125g butter, melted
300g fresh blueberries
Filling
250g cottage cheese
250g cream cheese
2 teaspoons finely grated
  lemon rind
¾ cup (165g) caster sugar
3 eggs
1 cup (240g) sour cream
¼ cup (60ml) lemon juice

1 Process biscuits until fine. Add butter, process until combined. Press mixture over base and side of 22cm springform tin. Place tin on oven tray; refrigerate 30 minutes.
2 Preheat oven to 160°C/140°C fan-forced.
3 Make filling by sieving cottage cheese into medium bowl; add cream cheese, rind and sugar. Beat with electric mixer until smooth; beat in eggs, one at a time, then sour cream and juice.
4 Pour filling into tin; bake about 1¼ hours. Cool in oven with door ajar.
5 Refrigerate cheesecake 3 hours or overnight.
6 Top cheesecake with blueberries. Dust with sifted icing sugar, if desired.

Serves 12

¾ cup (110g) plain flour
¼ teaspoon ground cinnamon
pinch ground nutmeg
⅓ cup (75g) caster sugar
80g butter, melted
½ teaspoon vanilla extract
⅓ cup (45g) roasted hazelnuts,
    chopped coarsely
¼ cup (80g) apricot jam,
    warmed, strained

Filling
1 vanilla bean
250g cream cheese, softened
500g ricotta cheese
2 tablespoons lemon juice
⅔ cup (150g) caster sugar
2 eggs

1 Grease 24cm springform tin.
2 Sift flour, spices and sugar into medium bowl; stir in butter, extract and nuts. Press mixture over base of tin. Place tin on oven tray; refrigerate 30 minutes.
3 Preheat oven to 180°C/160°C fan-forced.
4 Bake base about 20 minutes or until browned lightly. Spread with jam. Reduce oven temperature to 150°C/130°C fan-forced.
5 Make filling by splitting vanilla bean in half lengthways; scrape seeds into medium bowl. Add cheeses, juice and half the sugar; beat, with electric mixer until combined. Beat remaining sugar and eggs in small bowl with electric mixer about 5 minutes or until thick and creamy; fold into cheese mixture.
6 Pour filling into tin; bake about 35 minutes. Cool cheesecake in oven with door ajar.
7 Refrigerate cheesecake 3 hours or overnight. Serve cheesecake with cream, if desired.

Serves 12

vanilla spice cheesecake

butterscotch pecan cheesecake

150g plain chocolate biscuits
50g butter, melted
Filling
500g cream cheese, softened
1 teaspoon vanilla extract
¾ cup (165g) caster sugar
2 eggs
1 tablespoon plain flour
½ cup (60g) roasted pecans,
   chopped finely
Butterscotch topping
⅓ cup (75g) firmly packed
   brown sugar
40g butter
1 tablespoon cream

1 Preheat oven to 160°C/140°C fan-forced.
2 Process biscuits until fine. Add butter, process until combined. Press mixture over base of 20cm springform tin. Place tin on oven tray; refrigerate 30 minutes.
3 Make filling by beating cheese, extract and sugar in medium bowl with electric mixer until smooth; beat in eggs. Stir in flour and nuts.
4 Pour filling into tin; bake about 45 minutes. Cool cheesecake in oven with door ajar.
5 Make butterscotch topping by heating ingredients in small saucepan until smooth.
6 Spread topping over cheesecake. Refrigerate 3 hours or overnight.

Serves 8

125g plain chocolate biscuits
75g butter, melted
Filling
425g can seeded black cherries
   in syrup, drained
500g cream cheese, softened
⅓ cup (75g) caster sugar
2 eggs
200g dark eating chocolate,
   melted
3 x 55g Cherry Ripe bars,
   chopped coarsely

1 Grease 24cm springform tin.
2 Process biscuits until fine. Add butter, process until combined. Press mixture over base of tin. Place tin on oven tray; refrigerate 30 minutes.
3 Preheat oven to 180°C/160°C fan-forced.
4 Make filling by placing cherries on absorbent paper. Beat cheese and sugar in medium bowl with electric mixer until smooth; beat in eggs, one at a time. Gradually beat in cooled chocolate; stir in Cherry Ripe and cherries.
5 Spread filling into tin; bake about 50 minutes. Cool in oven with door ajar.
6 Refrigerate cheesecake 3 hours or overnight. Serve topped with dark chocolate curls, if desired.

Serves 12

cherry-choc cheesecake

italian ricotta cheesecake

90g butter, softened
¼ cup (55g) caster sugar
1 egg
1¼ cups (185g) plain flour
¼ cup (35g) self-raising flour
Filling
1kg ricotta cheese
1 tablespoon finely grated
   lemon rind
¼ cup (60ml) lemon juice
1 cup (220g) caster sugar
5 eggs
¼ cup (40g) sultanas
¼ cup (80g) finely chopped
   glacé fruit salad

1 Grease 28cm springform tin.
2 Beat butter, sugar and egg in small bowl with electric mixer until combined.
3 Stir in half the sifted flours; then work in remaining flour with hand. Knead pastry lightly on floured surface until smooth, wrap in plastic; refrigerate 30 minutes.
4 Press pastry over base of tin; prick with fork. Place on oven tray; refrigerate 30 minutes.
5 Preheat oven to 200°C/180°C fan-forced.
6 Cover pastry with baking paper, fill with beans or rice; bake 10 minutes. Remove paper and beans; bake 15 minutes or until browned lightly. Cool.
7 Reduce oven temperature to 160°C/140°C fan-forced.
8 Make filling by processing cheese, rind, juice, sugar and eggs until smooth; stir in fruit.

9 Pour filling into tin; bake about 50 minutes. Cool cheesecake in oven with door ajar.
10 Refrigerate cheesecake 3 hours or overnight.
11 Serve cheesecake dusted with sifted icing sugar, if desired.

Serves 16

choc rum 'n' raisin cheesecake

⅓ cup (80ml) dark rum
1 cup (160g) coarsely
   chopped raisins
150g butter, chopped
100g dark eating chocolate,
   chopped coarsely
1 cup (220g) caster sugar
⅔ cup (160ml) water
1 cup (150g) plain flour
2 tablespoons cocoa powder
2 egg yolks
Filling
500g cream cheese, softened
½ cup (110g) caster sugar
3 eggs
250g dark eating chocolate,
   melted

1 Combine rum and raisins in small bowl, cover; stand 3 hours or overnight.

2 Preheat oven to 180°C/160°C fan-forced. Grease 20cm x 30cm lamington pan; line base with baking paper, extending paper 5cm over long sides.

3 Combine butter, chocolate, sugar and the water in medium saucepan; stir over low heat until smooth. Remove from heat; stir in sifted flour and cocoa, then egg yolks.

4 Pour mixture into pan; bake about 15 minutes. Cool in pan.

5 Make filling by beating cheese and sugar in medium bowl with electric mixer until smooth; beat in eggs, one at a time. Stir in cooled chocolate, then raisin mixture.

6 Pour filling over base; bake about 45 minutes. Cool cheesecake in oven with door ajar.

7 Refrigerate 3 hours or overnight. Serve dusted with sifted cocoa, if desired.

Serves 18

250g plain sweet biscuits
125g butter, melted
Filling
750g cream cheese,
    softened
2 teaspoons finely grated
    orange rind
1 teaspoon finely grated
    lemon rind
1 cup (220g) caster sugar
3 eggs
¾ cup (180g) sour cream
¼ cup (60ml) lemon juice
Sour cream topping
1 cup (240g) sour cream
2 tablespoons caster sugar
2 teaspoons lemon juice

1 Process biscuits until fine. Add butter, process until combined. Press mixture over base and side of 24cm springform tin. Place tin on oven tray; refrigerate 30 minutes.

2 Preheat oven to 180°C/160°C fan-forced.

3 Make filling by beating cheese, rinds and sugar in medium bowl with electric mixer until smooth. Beat in eggs, one at a time, then cream and juice.

4 Pour filling into tin; bake 1¼ hours. Remove from oven; cool 15 minutes.

5 Make sour cream topping by combining ingredients in small bowl; spread over cheesecake.

6 Bake cheesecake 20 minutes; cool in oven with door ajar.

7 Refrigerate cheesecake 3 hours or overnight.

Serves 12

new york cheesecake

200g low-fat cottage cheese
250g light spreadable
    cream cheese
2 teaspoons finely grated
    lemon rind
¾ cup (165g) caster sugar
2 eggs
⅓ cup (55g) semolina
¼ cup (35g) self-raising flour
¼ cup (60ml) buttermilk
200g fresh or frozen
    blackberries

1 Preheat oven to 160°C/140°C fan-forced. Grease 20cm springform tin; line base with baking paper. Place tin on oven tray.

2 Beat cheeses, rind and sugar in medium bowl with electric mixer until smooth; beat in eggs, one at a time. Stir in semolina and sifted flour, then buttermilk.

3 Pour mixture into tin, sprinkle with blackberries; bake about 1 hour. Cool cheesecake in oven with door ajar.

4 Refrigerate cheesecake 3 hours or overnight.

5 Serve dusted with sifted icing sugar, if desired.

Serves 12

low-fat lemon and blackberry cheesecake

sticky date cheesecake

2 cups (280g) seeded dried dates
¾ cup (180ml) water
½ teaspoon bicarbonate of soda
750g cream cheese, softened
½ cup (110g) firmly packed
   brown sugar
¼ teaspoon ground cinnamon
¼ teaspoon mixed spice
2 eggs
Caramel sauce
25g butter
⅓ cup (75g) firmly packed
   brown sugar
⅓ cup (80ml) cream

1 Preheat oven to 160°C/140°C fan-forced. Grease 24cm springform tin; line base and side with baking paper. Place tin on oven tray.
2 Combine dates, the water and soda in small saucepan; bring to a boil, simmer 5 minutes. Cool mixture 5 minutes; blend or process until almost smooth.
3 Beat cheese and sugar in medium bowl with electric mixer until smooth. Add spices, eggs and date mixture; beat until combined.
4 Pour mixture into tin; bake about 1 hour. Cool cheesecake in oven with door ajar.
5 Refrigerate cheesecake 3 hours or overnight.
6 Make caramel sauce.
7 Serve cheesecake drizzled with warm or cold sauce.

Caramel sauce
Combine ingredients in small saucepan; stir over low heat, until smooth. Bring to a boil; remove from heat.

Serves 12

jaffa liqueur cheesecake slice

250g plain chocolate biscuits
150g butter, melted
Filling
3 eggs
¾ cup (165g) caster sugar
500g cream cheese, softened
100g dark eating chocolate, melted
1 tablespoon finely grated orange rind
2 tablespoons Cointreau
Chocolate ganache
150g dark eating chocolate, chopped coarsely
¼ cup (60ml) cream

1 Grease 19cm x 29cm slice pan; line base with baking paper, extending paper 5cm over long sides.
2 Process biscuits until fine. Add butter; process until combined. Press mixture over base of pan; refrigerate 30 minutes.
3 Preheat oven to 160°C/140°C fan-forced.
4 Make filling by beating eggs and sugar in small bowl with electric mixer until thick and creamy. Beat cheese in medium bowl with electric mixer until smooth; beat in egg mixture in two batches.
5 Pour half the cheese mixture into another medium bowl. Stir cooled chocolate into one bowl, and rind and Cointreau into the other bowl. Pour both mixtures into pan, swirl with skewer; bake about 25 minutes. Cool cheesecake in oven with door ajar.
6 Make chocolate ganache.
7 Spread ganache over cheesecake; refrigerate 3 hours or overnight.

Chocolate ganache
Combine ingredients in small saucepan; stir over low heat until smooth. Cool 10 minutes.

Serves 12

250g plain sweet biscuits
125g butter, melted
Filling
500g cream cheese, softened
½ cup (110g) firmly packed
   brown sugar
2 teaspoons vanilla extract
1 teaspoon mixed spice
½ cup (125ml) cream
3 egg yolks
2 egg whites
Honey syrup
2 cinnamon sticks
4 strips lemon rind
⅓ cup (120g) honey
1 tablespoon water
¾ teaspoon gelatine

1 Grease deep 19cm square cake pan; line base and sides with baking paper, extending paper 5cm above edges of pan.
2 Process biscuits until fine; add butter, process until combined. Press mixture over base of pan; refrigerate 30 minutes.
3 Preheat oven to 160°C/140°C fan-forced.
4 Make filling by beating cheese, sugar, extract and spice in medium bowl with electric mixer until smooth; beat in cream and egg yolks.
5 Beat egg whites in small bowl with electric mixer until soft peaks form; fold into cream cheese mixture.
6 Pour filling into pan; bake about 50 minutes. Cool cheesecake in oven with door ajar.
7 Refrigerate cheesecake 3 hours or overnight.
8 Make honey syrup.
9 Serve cheesecake with warm syrup.

Honey syrup
Combine ingredients in small saucepan, bring to a boil; remove from heat.

Serves 9

mixed spice cheesecake with honey syrup

orange and roasted plum tart

1½ cups (225g) plain flour
¼ cup (40g) icing sugar
125g cold butter, chopped
2 egg yolks
1 tablespoon iced water
8 small plums (560g), quartered
2 tablespoons orange juice
2 tablespoons brown sugar
Filling
500g cream cheese, softened
1 tablespoon finely grated
    orange rind
⅔ cup (150g) caster sugar
2 eggs
½ cup (120g) sour cream
2 tablespoons plain flour
⅓ cup (80ml) orange juice

1 Grease 19cm x 27cm rectangular loose-based flan tin or 26cm springform tin.
2 Process flour, icing sugar and butter until crumbly. Add egg yolks and the water; pulse until ingredients come together. Knead pastry on floured surface until smooth. Wrap in plastic; refrigerate 30 minutes.
3 Roll pastry between sheets of baking paper until large enough to line tin; press into sides, trim edges. Refrigerate 30 minutes.
4 Preheat oven to 180°C/160°C fan-forced.
5 Cover pastry with baking paper, fill with dried beans or rice; place on oven tray. Bake 10 minutes. Remove paper and beans; bake 10 minutes or until pastry is browned lightly. Cool.
6 Reduce oven temperature to 160°C/140°C fan-forced.
7 Make filling.
8 Pour filling into tin; bake about 50 minutes. Cool tart; refrigerate 3 hours.

9 Increase oven temperature to 200°C/180°C fan-forced. Place plums in single layer on oven tray, sprinkle with juice and sugar. Roast plums about 20 minutes or until soft. Cool.
10 Serve tart topped with roasted plums.

Filling
Beat cheese, rind and sugar in medium bowl with electric mixer until smooth. Beat in eggs, one at a time. Add remaining ingredients; beat until smooth.

Serves 8

cinnamon and apple cheesecake

1 sheet ready-rolled
   shortcrust pastry
2 medium golden delicious
   apples (300g), unpeeled,
   sliced thinly
1 tablespoon lemon juice
1 tablespoon demerara sugar
Filling
750g cream cheese, softened
¾ cup (165g) caster sugar
1 teaspoon ground cinnamon
3 eggs, separated
¾ cup (180ml) cream

1 Preheat oven to 180°C/160°C fan-forced. Grease 24cm springform tin; place on oven tray.

2 Cut pastry into 24cm round, place in tin; prick well with a fork. Bake about 20 minutes or until browned lightly. Cool 5 minutes.

3 Make filling by beating cheese, sugar, cinnamon and egg yolks in medium bowl with electric mixer until smooth; beat in cream. Beat egg whites in small bowl with electric mixer until soft peaks form; fold into cheese mixture in two batches. Pour filling into tin.

4 Combine apple slices and lemon juice in small bowl. Arrange slices, slightly overlapping, over filling; sprinkle with sugar.

5 Bake about 50 minutes. Cool in oven with door ajar.

6 Refrigerate cheesecake 3 hours or overnight.

Serves 12

celebration cheesecake

500g fruit cake, cut into
  1cm slices
1 medium pink grapefruit (425g),
  segmented
2 large oranges (600g),
  segmented
250g strawberries, halved
120g fresh raspberries
150g fresh blueberries
Filling
750g cream cheese, softened
300g sour cream
1 teaspoon vanilla extract
1 cup (220g) caster sugar
¼ cup (60ml) brandy
½ teaspoon ground nutmeg
3 eggs
Toffee
1 cup (220g) caster sugar
1 cup (250ml) water

1 Preheat oven to 180°C/160°C fan-forced. Grease 26cm springform tin; line base with baking paper.
2 Cover base of tin with cake slices; bake 10 minutes. Reduce oven temperature to 150°C/130°C fan-forced.
3 Make filling by beating cheese, sour cream, extract, sugar, brandy and nutmeg in large bowl with electric mixer until smooth. Beat in eggs, one at a time.
4 Pour filling into tin; bake about 45 minutes. Cool in oven with door ajar.
5 Refrigerate cheesecake 3 hours or overnight.
6 Make toffee.
7 Remove cheesecake from tin, to serving plate; top with fruit. Drizzle toffee over fruit.

Toffee
Stir sugar and the water in medium heavy-based frying pan over high heat until sugar dissolves. Boil, without stirring, uncovered, 10 minutes or until mixture is golden brown in colour. Remove from heat; stand until bubbles subside before using.

Serves 16

100g plain sweet biscuits
50g butter, melted
150g frozen cranberries
Filling
¼ cup (60ml) thickened cream
180g white eating chocolate,
　chopped coarsely
375g cream cheese, softened
1 teaspoon finely grated
　orange rind
½ cup (110g) caster sugar
1 egg

1 Preheat oven to 150°C/130°C fan-forced. Line 6-hole texas (¾ cup/180ml) muffin pan with paper cases or freeform cases, made from 17cm square sheets of baking paper. (You can also use a 22cm springform tin.)

2 Process biscuits until fine. Add butter, process until combined. Divide mixture among paper cases; press firmly over base of pan. Refrigerate 30 minutes.

3 Make filling by combining cream and 130g of the chocolate in small saucepan; stir over low heat until smooth.

4 Beat cheese, rind, sugar and egg in small bowl with electric mixer until smooth. Stir in cooled chocolate mixture.

5 Divide mixture among cases, sprinkle with cranberries. Bake about 30 minutes. Cool in oven with door ajar.

6 Refrigerate cheesecakes 3 hours.

7 Melt remaining chocolate; drizzle over cheesecakes.

Makes 6

white chocolate and cranberry cheesecakes

triple coconut cheesecake

90g coconut macaroons
125g plain sweet biscuits
125g butter, melted
Filling
250g cream cheese, softened
½ cup (110g) caster sugar
300g sour cream
2 tablespoons Malibu
2 x 140ml cans coconut milk
½ cup (40g) desiccated coconut,
  roasted
¼ cup (35g) cornflour
3 eggs
Glaze
100g dark eating chocolate,
  chopped coarsely
60g unsalted butter, chopped

1 Preheat oven to 160°C/140°C fan-forced.
2 Process macaroons and biscuits until fine. Add butter, process until combined. Press mixture over base and side of 26cm springform tin. Place tin on oven tray; refrigerate 30 minutes.
3 Make filling by beating cheese, sugar, sour cream, Malibu, coconut milk, coconut and cornflour in medium bowl with electric mixer until smooth. Beat in eggs, one at a time.
4 Pour filling into tin; bake about 1 hour. Cool cheesecake in oven with door ajar.
5 Refrigerate cheesecake 3 hours or overnight.
6 Make glaze.
7 Spread glaze over cheesecake; stand 20 minutes before serving.

Glaze
Combine ingredients in small saucepan; stir over low heat until smooth. Refrigerate until mixture is spreadable.

Serves 12

125g butter, chopped
150g dark eating chocolate,
    chopped coarsely
1 egg
⅔ cup (150g) caster sugar
¾ cup (110g) plain flour
¼ cup (35g) self-raising flour
Topping
250g cream cheese, softened
1 teaspoon vanilla extract
⅓ cup (75g) caster sugar
1 egg
½ cup (125ml) cream

1 Preheat oven to 180°C/160°C fan-forced. Grease deep 19cm-square cake pan; line base and sides with baking paper, extending paper 5cm over edge of sides.
2 Combine butter and chocolate in small saucepan; stir over low heat until smooth. Cool.
3 Beat egg and sugar in small bowl with electric mixer until thick and creamy. Stir in chocolate mixture and sifted flours.
4 Spread mixture into pan; bake 10 minutes.
5 Make topping.
6 Pour topping over brownie base; bake about 15 minutes. Cool in oven with door ajar.
7 Refrigerate brownies 3 hours.
8 Serve topped with fresh raspberries, if desired.

Topping
Beat cheese, extract, sugar and egg in small bowl with electric mixer until smooth; beat in cream.

Serves 12

cheesecake brownies

spiced fig and orange cheesecake

½ cup (80g) brazil nuts
125g plain sweet biscuits
80g butter, melted
1 cup (250ml) orange juice
1¼ cups (250g) finely chopped
   dried figs
1 cinnamon stick
pinch ground clove
Filling
250g cream cheese, softened
1 tablespoon finely grated
   orange rind
¾ cup (165g) caster sugar
1 cup (250g) mascarpone
2 eggs, separated

1 Grease 22cm springform tin.
2 Process nuts and biscuits until fine. Add butter; process until combined. Press mixture over base of tin. Place tin on oven tray; refrigerate 30 minutes.
3 Preheat oven to 160°C/140°C fan-forced.
4 Combine juice, figs, cinnamon and cloves in small saucepan; simmer, uncovered, 10 minutes or until most of the juice has been absorbed. Discard cinnamon stick. Spread fig mixture over crumb base in tin.
5 Make filling by beating cream cheese, rind and sugar in medium bowl with electric mixer until smooth. Add mascarpone and yolks; beat only until combined. Beat egg whites in small bowl with electric mixer until soft peaks form; fold into cheese mixture.

6 Pour filling over fig mixture; bake about 1¼ hours. Cool in oven with door ajar.
7 Refrigerate cheesecake 3 hours or overnight. Serve dusted with sifted icing sugar, if desired.

Serves 12

250g plain sweet biscuits
125g butter, melted
½ teaspoon mixed spice
Filling
4 eggs
¾ cup (165g) caster sugar
500g cream cheese
1 tablespoon finely grated
   lemon rind

1 Process biscuits until fine. Add butter, process until combined. Press mixture over base and sides of 20cm springform tin. Place tin on oven tray; refrigerate 30 minutes.
2 Preheat oven to 160°C/140°C fan-forced.
3 Make filling by beating eggs and sugar in small bowl with electric mixer until thick and creamy. Beat cheese and rind in medium bowl with electric mixer until smooth. Add egg mixture to cheese mixture; beat until combined.
4 Pour filling into tin; bake about 50 minutes. Cool in oven with door ajar. Refrigerate 3 hours or overnight.
5 Serve cheesecake sprinkled with mixed spice.

Serves 10

bistro cheesecake

black forest cheesecake slice

425g can seedless black
cherries in syrup
200g dark eating chocolate,
melted
125g cream cheese, softened
125g mascarpone
½ cup (110g) caster sugar
⅔ cup (160ml) cream
1 egg, separated
Cherry topping
85g packet cherry flavoured
jelly crystals
⅔ cup (160ml) boiling water

1 Preheat oven to 160°C/140°C
fan-forced. Grease base of
19cm x 29cm slice pan; line base
with baking paper, extending
paper 5cm over long sides.
2 Drain cherries; reserve syrup.
Make cherry topping.
3 Spread chocolate over base
of pan; refrigerate until set.
4 Beat cheese, mascarpone,
sugar, cream and egg yolk in
small bowl with electric mixer
until smooth; stir in cherries.
5 Beat egg white in small bowl
with electric mixer until soft
peaks form; fold into cream
cheese mixture. Pour over
chocolate base.
6 Bake about 35 minutes; cool
in oven with door ajar.
7 Pour topping over cheesecake.
Refrigerate overnight.

Cherry topping
Combine jelly crystals and the
water in small bowl, stir until
jelly is dissolved. Stir in ⅔ cup
reserved cherry syrup; cool.
Refrigerate jelly until thickened
to the stage where it resembles
unbeaten eggwhites.

Serves 8

2 sheets ready-rolled puff pastry
1 tablespoon almond meal
1 egg white
1 tablespoon demerara sugar
Filling
250g cream cheese, softened
2 tablespoons caster sugar
2 tablespoons plain flour
1 egg
Topping
6 large stems (375g) trimmed
  rhubarb, cut into three
  crossways
¼ cup (55g) demerara sugar
2 tablespoons Grand Marnier

1 Preheat oven to 200°C/180°C fan-forced.
2 Make topping.
3 Cut one pastry sheet into 14cm x 24cm rectangle; cut remaining sheet into 18cm x 24cm rectangle. Leaving 2cm border around all sides, make about seven slits across width of larger sheet. Place smaller sheet on greased oven tray; sprinkle with almond meal.
4 Make filling by beating cheese and sugar in small bowl with electric mixer until smooth. Beat in flour and egg. Spread filling over pastry on tray leaving 2cm border around edges; spread with topping. Brush around border with egg white, place remaining pastry over filling; press edges together to seal.
5 Brush pastry with egg white; sprinkle with sugar. Bake about 30 minutes or until jalousie is browned lightly. Stand 1 hour before serving.

Topping
Combine ingredients in large frying pan; cook, stirring gently, until rhubarb softens. Cool.

Serves 8

rhubarb and almond jalousie

⅓ cup (80ml) vegetable oil
⅓ cup (75g) firmly packed
   brown sugar
1 egg
¾ cup (110g) self-raising flour
½ teaspoon mixed spice
1 cup (40g) coarsely
   grated carrot
½ cup (55g) coarsely
   chopped walnuts
Filling
750g cream cheese, softened
2 teaspoons finely grated
   orange rind
¾ cup (165g) caster sugar
3 eggs
2 tablespoons plain flour
½ teaspoon mixed spice
½ teaspoon ground cardamom
1 cup (40g) finely grated carrot

1 Preheat oven to 160°C/140°C fan-forced. Grease 23cm square cake pan; line base and sides with baking paper, extending paper 5cm above edges of pan.
2 Beat oil, sugar and egg in small bowl with electric mixer, until thick and creamy. Stir in sifted flour and spice, carrot and nuts.
3 Spread mixture into pan; bake 15 minutes. Remove from oven; stand 15 minutes.
4 Make filling by beating cheese, rind and sugar in medium bowl with electric mixer until smooth. Beat in eggs, one at a time. Stir in sifted flour and spices, then carrot.
5 Pour filling over cake base; bake about 40 minutes. Cool in oven with door ajar.
6 Refrigerate cheesecake 3 hours or overnight.
7 Serve cheesecake sprinkled with extra mixed spice, if desired.

Serves 12

spicy carrot and walnut cheesecake

150g butternut snap biscuits
75g butter, melted
¼ cup (60g) finely chopped
   glacé ginger
½ cup (115g) finely chopped
   glacé pineapple
Filling
500g cream cheese, softened
½ cup (110g) caster sugar
½ cup (120g) sour cream
2 tablespoons plain flour
3 eggs

1 Grease 24cm springform tin; line base and side with baking paper.
2 Process biscuits until fine. Add butter, process until combined. Press mixture over base of tin. Place tin on oven tray; refrigerate 30 minutes.
3 Preheat oven to 160°C/140°C fan-forced.
4 Make filling by beating cheese, sugar, cream and flour in medium bowl with electric mixer until smooth; beat in eggs, one at a time.
5 Combine ginger and pineapple; sprinkle one-third over base. Pour filling over fruit; bake 15 minutes. Sprinkle with remaining fruit; bake about 35 minutes. Cool in oven with door ajar.
6 Refrigerate cheesecake 3 hours or overnight.

Serves 12

glacé ginger and pineapple cheesecake

125g granita biscuits
80g butter, melted
Filling
1 vanilla bean
500g cream cheese, softened
1½ cups (330g) caster sugar
2 eggs
½ cup (120g) sour cream
¼ cup (60ml) lemon juice
Poached quince
1 cup (220g) caster sugar
2 cups (500ml) water
2 medium quinces (700g),
    peeled, cored, quartered
2 strips lemon rind

1 Process biscuits until fine. Add butter; process until combined. Press mixture over base of 24cm springform tin. Place tin on oven tray; refrigerate 30 minutes.

2 Preheat oven to 160°C/140°C fan-forced.

3 Make filling by splitting vanilla bean in half lengthways, then scrape seeds into medium bowl; reserve pod for poached quinces. Add cheese, sugar, eggs, sour cream and juice to bowl; beat with electric mixer until smooth.

4 Pour filling into tin; bake about 35 minutes. Cool cheesecake in oven with door ajar. Refrigerate 3 hours or overnight.

5 Make poached quince.

6 Top cheesecake with quince; brush with quince syrup.

Poached quince
Stir sugar and the water in medium saucepan over heat until sugar dissolves. Add quince, rind and reserved vanilla pod; simmer, covered, about 2 hours or until quince is tender and rosy in colour. Cool quince in syrup. Remove quince from syrup; slice thinly. Simmer syrup, uncovered, until reduced by about half; cool.

Serves 12

vanilla cheesecake with poached quince

chilled cheesecakes

Non-baked cheesecakes surprise with each bite
– they're light and mousse-like, yet rich and creamy.
Suitably special for a summer dinner party and
delicious enough to eat all year round.

180g coconut macaroons
60g butter, melted
Filling
1½ teaspoons gelatine
2 tablespoons water
250g cream cheese, softened
¼ cup (55g) caster sugar
1 cup (250ml) cream
¼ cup (60ml) Malibu
Pineapple topping
1 cup (250ml) pineapple juice
¼ small pineapple (225g),
   halved lengthways,
   sliced thinly

1 Grease 12-hole (¼ cup/60ml) mini cheesecake pan with removable bases.
2 Process macaroons until fine. Add butter; process until combined. Press a heaped tablespoon of mixture over base of each hole in pan. Refrigerate 30 minutes.
3 Make filling by sprinkling gelatine over the water in small heatproof jug; stand jug in small saucepan of simmering water. Stir until gelatine dissolves; cool 5 minutes.
4 Beat cheese and sugar in small bowl with electric mixer until smooth; beat in cream. Stir in Malibu and gelatine mixture. Divide mixture over bases; refrigerate overnight.
5 Make pineapple topping.
6 Serve cheesecakes topped with pineapple and juice.

Pineapple topping
Combine juice and pineapple in medium frying pan; simmer, about 10 minutes or until pineapple is soft. Remove pineapple from juice; simmer juice about 5 minutes or until thickened slightly. Cool.

Makes 12

pineapple and coconut cheesecakes

berry bombe cheesecakes

450g madeira cake
2 teaspoons gelatine
2 tablespoons water
375g cream cheese, softened
½ cup (110g) caster sugar
300ml cream
1 cup (130g) frozen blackberries
1 tablespoon lemon juice
Meringue
4 egg whites
¾ cup (165g) caster sugar
1 teaspoon cornflour

1 Line 5-cup capacity pudding basin or bowl with plastic wrap, extending plastic 5cm over edge of basin.
2 Trim brown edges from cake. Cut two 1cm slices, lengthways, from cake; reserve remaining cake. Place cake slices together; cut out a 15cm round to fit the top of basin. Crumble remaining cake into basin; press crumbs firmly over base and side of basin.
3 Sprinkle gelatine over the water in small heatproof jug; stand jug in small saucepan of simmering water. Stir until gelatine dissolves. Cool 5 minutes.
4 Beat cheese and sugar in small bowl with electric mixer until smooth; beat in cream. Stir in gelatine mixture, then blackberries and juice. Pour mixture into basin; top with cake round. Cover with plastic wrap; refrigerate overnight.

5 Preheat oven to 240°C/220°C fan-forced.
6 Make meringue.
7 Turn cheesecake onto oven tray; discard plastic wrap. Spread meringue over bombe to enclose completely. Bake 3 minutes or until browned lightly. Serve immediately.

Meringue
Beat egg whites in small bowl with electric mixer until soft peaks form; gradually add sugar, beating between additions until sugar dissolves. Fold in cornflour.

Serves 8

sticky rhubarb on citrus cheesecakes

250g plain sweet biscuits
125g butter, melted
¼ teaspoon ground nutmeg
Filling
4 eggs, separated
1 cup (220g) caster sugar
2 tablespoons finely grated
   lemon rind
½ cup (125ml) lemon juice
½ cup (125ml) orange juice
1½ tablespoons gelatine
½ cup (125ml) water
500g cream cheese, softened
300ml thickened cream,
   whipped
Sticky rhubarb
8 large stems (500g) trimmed
   rhubarb, cut into 5cm lengths
¾ cup (165g) caster sugar
2 teaspoons lemon juice

1 Start making sticky rhubarb by standing rhubarb and sugar mixture overnight.
2 Grease eight 10cm round springform tins or 28cm springform tin; place on tray.
3 Process or blend biscuits until fine. Add butter and nutmeg; process until combined. Press mixture over base of tins. Refrigerate 30 minutes.
4 Make filling by combining egg yolks, sugar, rind and juices in medium heatproof bowl; whisk over medium saucepan of simmering water about 10 minutes or until thick and foamy. Remove from heat.
5 Sprinkle gelatine over the water in small heatproof jug; stand jug in small saucepan of simmering water. Stir until gelatine dissolves; stir into egg yolk mixture. Cool.
6 Beat cheese in large bowl with electric mixer until smooth; beat in egg yolk mixture in four batches.

7 Beat egg whites in small bowl, with electric mixer until soft peaks form. Fold whipped cream into cheese mixture, then fold in egg whites in two batches. Divide mixture among tins. Refrigerate overnight.
8 Remove rhubarb mixture from refrigerator; continue making sticky rhubarb.
9 Serve cheesecakes topped with sticky rhubarb.

Sticky rhubarb
Combine rhubarb and sugar in colander, stand colander in a bowl; refrigerate overnight. Combine rhubarb and drained liquid in large frying pan; simmer, uncovered about 5 minutes or until rhubarb has softened. Fold in juice; cool.

Makes 8

12 savoiardi sponge
    finger biscuits
½ cup (155g) strawberry jam,
    warmed
2 tablespoons hot water
350g strawberries
¼ cup (80g) strawberry jam,
    warmed, strained, extra
1 tablespoon lemon juice
Filling
1 tablespoon gelatine
¼ cup (60ml) water
500g low-fat ricotta cheese
1 teaspoon finely grated
    lemon rind
¼ cup (55g) caster sugar
300ml low-fat cream
2 teaspoons lemon juice
3 egg whites

1 Grease base of deep 19cm square cake pan; line base and sides with plastic wrap, extending wrap 5cm over sides of pan. Trim one round edge from each biscuit. Place biscuits in single layer over base of pan; brush with combined jam and the hot water.

2 Make filling by sprinkling gelatine over the water in small heatproof jug; stand jug in small saucepan of simmering water. Stir until gelatine dissolves; cool 5 minutes.

3 Beat ricotta, rind and sugar in medium bowl with electric mixer until smooth; beat in cream and juice. Stir in gelatine mixture.

4 Beat egg whites in small bowl with electric mixer until soft peaks form; fold into ricotta mixture in two batches.

5 Pour filling over base. Refrigerate overnight.

6 Serve cheesecake topped with strawberries, brushed with combined extra jam and juice.

Serves 9

low-fat strawberries and cream cheesecake

almond praline cheesecake

100g butter, softened
2 tablespoons caster sugar
2 tablespoons rice flour
½ cup (75g) plain flour
Filling
2 teaspoons gelatine
2 tablespoons water
375g cream cheese, softened
½ cup (110g) caster sugar
300ml cream
1 teaspoon vanilla extract
Almond praline
½ cup (110g) caster sugar
¼ cup (60ml) water
¼ cup (35g) slivered almonds,
 roasted

1 Preheat oven to 150°C/130°C fan-forced. Grease 22cm springform tin.
2 Beat butter and sugar in small bowl with electric mixer until light and fluffy. Stir in sifted flours in two batches; knead on lightly floured surface until smooth.
3 Press mixture evenly over base of tin; bake shortbread about 35 minutes or until browned lightly. Cool in tin.
4 Make almond praline.
5 Remove base and shortbread from tin. Line tin with plastic wrap (see page 353). Replace base and shortbread; secure tin. Pull plastic wrap firmly up side of tin.
6 Make filling by sprinkling gelatine over the water in small heatproof jug; stand jug in small saucepan of simmering water. Stir until gelatine dissolves. Cool 5 minutes.
7 Beat cheese and sugar in medium bowl with electric mixer until smooth; beat in cream and extract. Stir in gelatine mixture. Finely chop praline; stir half into cheese mixture. Pour into tin; refrigerate overnight.
8 Serve cheesecake topped with remaining praline.

Almond praline
Combine sugar and the water in small saucepan; stir over low heat until sugar dissolves. Boil about 10 minutes or until mixture turns golden brown. Remove from heat. Place nuts in single layer on greased oven tray. Pour toffee over almonds. Stand at room temperature 10 minutes or until set.

Serves 10

date cheesecake roll

2 tablespoons white sugar
1 cup (140g) seeded
   dried dates
¾ cup (180ml) boiling water
1 teaspoon bicarbonate of soda
50g butter, chopped
⅔ cup (165g) firmly packed
   brown sugar
2 eggs
¾ cup (110g) self-raising flour
Filling
1 teaspoon gelatine
1 tablespoon water
250g cream cheese, softened
½ cup (125ml) cream
2 tablespoons caster sugar
Butterscotch filling
½ cup (110g) firmly packed
   brown sugar
⅓ cup (80ml) cream
50g butter, chopped

1 Make butterscotch filling.
2 Preheat oven to 180°C/160°C fan-forced. Grease 25cm x 30cm swiss roll pan; line base with baking paper, extending paper 5cm over long sides. Place a piece of baking paper cut the same size as swiss roll pan on bench; sprinkle evenly with white sugar.
3 Combine dates, the water and soda in bowl of food processor, cover with lid; stand 5 minutes. Add butter and brown sugar; process until almost smooth. Add eggs and flour; pulse until combined.
4 Pour mixture into pan; bake about 15 minutes. Turn cake onto sugared paper, peel baking paper away; cut away crisp edges from all sides of cake.
5 Gently roll cake loosely, with the paper, from a long side; hold for 30 seconds, then unroll. Cover flat cake with tea towel; cool.
6 Make filling by sprinkling gelatine over the water in small heatproof jug; stand jug in small saucepan of simmering water. Stir until gelatine dissolves. Cool 5 minutes.

7 Beat cheese, cream and sugar in small bowl with electric mixer until smooth. Stir in gelatine mixture.
8 Spread cake with filling; dollop with butterscotch filling. Roll cake, by lifting paper and using it as a guide to roll.
9 Wrap roll in baking paper, then foil; place on tray. Refrigerate overnight before cutting.

Butterscotch filling
Combine ingredients in small saucepan, stir over heat until smooth; simmer, uncovered, about 10 minutes or until mixture thickens. Cool.

Serves 12

250g cream cheese, softened
1 teaspoon finely grated
    lime rind
⅔ cup (150g) caster sugar
300ml cream
¾ cup (180g) sour cream
green food colouring
¾ cup (180ml) lime juice
⅓ cup (80ml) orange juice
¼ cup (60ml) tequila
1 tablespoon Cointreau
¼ cup (55g) white sugar

1 Refrigerate eight ¾-cup (180ml) glasses.
2 Beat cheese, rind and caster sugar in small bowl with electric mixer until smooth. Add cream, sour cream and enough food colouring to tint mixture pale green; beat until smooth. Stir in juices, tequila and Cointreau.
3 Transfer mixture to large jug. Divide mixture among glasses; freeze overnight.
4 Place white sugar on saucer. Dip rim of glasses in cold water then into white sugar; serve immediately.

Serves 8

margarita cheesecakes

250g ginger nut biscuits
125g butter, melted
Filling
3 teaspoons gelatine
¼ cup (60ml) water
250g cream cheese
750g ricotta cheese
1 tablespoon finely grated
  lemon rind
½ cup (110g) caster sugar
⅓ cup (80ml) lemon juice
300ml thickened cream,
  whipped
Passionfruit topping
½ cup (125ml) orange juice
2 tablespoons passionfruit pulp
1 tablespoon caster sugar
2 teaspoons gelatine

1 Process biscuits until fine. Add butter, process until combined. Press mixture over base of 26cm springform tin. Refrigerate 30 minutes.
2 Make filling by sprinkling gelatine over the water in small heatproof jug; stand jug in small saucepan of simmering water. Stir until gelatine dissolves; cool 5 minutes.
3 Beat cheeses, rind, sugar and juice in large bowl with electric mixer until smooth. Stir in gelatine mixture; fold in cream. Spread filling into tin; refrigerate overnight.
4 Make passionfruit topping.
5 Pour topping over cheesecake. Refrigerate until set.

Passionfruit topping
Combine juice, passionfruit and sugar in small saucepan; stir over low heat until sugar is dissolved. Remove from heat; add gelatine, stir until dissolved. Cool 15 minutes.

Serves 16

lemon ricotta cheesecake

cookies and cream cheesecakes

You need an 80cm length of 50mm diameter PVC pipe, cut into 10cm lengths; ask the hardware store to do this for you, or use a hacksaw. This recipe will also fit into a 24cm springform tin. In this case, use a plain chocolate biscuit base (see page 131).

2 x 150g packets chocolate, cream-filled biscuits
50g dark eating chocolate, melted

Filling

2 teaspoons gelatine
2 tablespoons water
375g cream cheese, softened
1 teaspoon vanilla extract
½ cup (110g) caster sugar
300ml cream
180g white eating chocolate, melted

1 Stand eight cleaned 10cm lengths of PVC pipes on tray; grease each pipe and line with baking paper.
2 Place one biscuit in each pipe. Chop remaining biscuits into quarters.
3 Make filling by sprinkling gelatine over the water in small heatproof jug; stand jug in small saucepan of simmering water. Stir until gelatine dissolves; cool 5 minutes.
4 Beat cheese, extract and sugar in medium bowl with electric mixer until smooth; beat in cream. Stir in white chocolate, gelatine mixture and reserved biscuits.
5 Divide filling among pipes; refrigerate overnight.
6 Remove pipes and paper from cheesecakes; serve topped with chocolate.

Makes 8

roasted pear and almond tart

250g butternut snap biscuits
50g flaked almonds
125g butter, melted
Filling
2 teaspoons gelatine
2 tablespoons water
250g cream cheese, softened
⅓ cup (75g) caster sugar
¼ cup (90g) golden syrup
300ml thickened cream,
    whipped
Roasted pears
5 corella pears (500g), peeled,
    halved lengthways
⅓ cup (115g) golden syrup
30g butter

1 Grease 11cm x 34cm rectangular loose-based flan tin or 22cm springform tin.
2 Process biscuits and almonds until fine. Add butter; process until combined. Press mixture over base and side of tin. Refrigerate 30 minutes.
3 Make filling by sprinkling gelatine over the water in small heatproof jug; stand jug in small saucepan of simmering water. Stir until gelatine dissolves. Cool 5 minutes.
4 Beat cheese, sugar and golden syrup in small bowl with electric mixer until smooth. Stir in gelatine mixture; fold in cream. Pour filling into tin; refrigerate overnight.
5 Make roasted pears.
6 Serve cheesecake topped with pears and syrup.

Roasted pears
Preheat oven to 200°C/180°C fan-forced. Place pears in single layer, in large shallow baking dish; drizzle with golden syrup, dot with butter. Roast, uncovered, about 30 minutes, turning occasionally or until pears are soft. Cool to room temperature.

Serves 8

100g sponge cake,
  chopped coarsely
⅓ cup (80ml) Cointreau
300g frozen mixed berries
Filling
1 teaspoon gelatine
1 tablespoon water
250g cream cheese, softened
⅔ cup (150g) caster sugar
2 teaspoons lemon juice
300ml cream
Custard
¼ cup (30g) custard powder
¼ cup (55g) caster sugar
1½ cups (375ml) milk
20g butter
1 egg yolk

1 Divide sponge cake among eight 1⅓-cup (330ml) glasses; sprinkle with Cointreau and half of the berries.
2 Make filling by sprinkling gelatine over the water in small heatproof jug; stand jug in small saucepan of simmering water. Stir until gelatine dissolves; cool 5 minutes.
3 Beat cheese, sugar and juice in small bowl with electric mixer until smooth; beat in cream. Stir in gelatine mixture.
4 Divide mixture among glasses; top with remaining berries. Refrigerate 15 minutes.
5 Make custard.
6 Divide custard among glasses; refrigerate 30 minutes. Serve topped with fresh raspberries and blueberries, if desired.

Custard
Blend custard powder and sugar with ⅓ cup of the milk in small saucepan until smooth; stir in remaining milk. Stir over heat until mixture boils and thickens; remove from heat, stir in butter and egg yolk. Cover surface of custard with plastic wrap. Cool.

Serves 8

berry cheesecake trifles

½ cup (70g) roasted
   macadamia nuts
4 egg whites
¾ cup (165g) caster sugar
Filling
2 teaspoons gelatine
2 tablespoons water
250g cream cheese, softened
½ cup (110g) caster sugar
1 tablespoon lemon juice
300ml cream
Mango jelly
2 cups (500ml) mango puree
1 tablespoon gelatine

1 Preheat oven to 180°C/160°C fan-forced. Grease two 22cm springform tins; line bases and sides with baking paper.

2 Process half the nuts until fine. Chop remaining nuts coarsely.

3 Beat egg whites in small bowl with electric mixer until soft peaks form. Add sugar, 1 tablespoon at a time, beating until sugar dissolves between each addition. Fold in all nuts. Divide meringue between tins; bake 30 minutes. Cool meringues in oven with door ajar.

4 Make mango jelly.

5 Make filling by sprinkling gelatine over the water in small heatproof jug; stand jug in small saucepan of simmering water. Stir until gelatine dissolves; cool 5 minutes.

6 Beat cheese, sugar and juice in small bowl with electric mixer until smooth; beat in cream. Stir in gelatine mixture.

7 Remove paper collar from one of the meringue layers in tin. Line tin with plastic wrap (see page 353). Return meringue to tin, flatten with hand. Pour half the filling over meringue; refrigerate 15 minutes. Spread jelly over filling; cover, refrigerate 20 minutes. Spread remaining filling over jelly.

8 Remove remaining meringue and paper from tin. Place on top of cheesecake; press down gently. Refrigerate overnight.

Mango jelly
Place puree in small saucepan, sprinkle with gelatine; stir over low heat until gelatine is dissolved. Cool.

Serves 12

mango macadamia meringue cheesecake

250g chocolate chip biscuits
50g butter, melted
1 tablespoon milk
Filling
¾ cup (210g) crunchy
    peanut butter
½ cup (125ml) cream
250g cream cheese, softened
½ cup (110g) caster sugar
Hot chocolate sauce
200g dark eating chocolate,
    chopped coarsely
20g butter
½ cup (125ml) cream

1 Grease 24cm round loose-based flan tin.
2 Process biscuits until fine; add butter and milk, process until combined. Press mixture over base and side of tin. Freeze 30 minutes.
3 Make filling by combining peanut butter and cream in small saucepan; stir, over low heat until smooth. Cool.
4 Beat cheese and sugar in small bowl with electric mixer until smooth. Stir in peanut butter mixture.
5 Spread filling over crust; cover with foil, freeze 3 hours or overnight.
6 Make hot chocolate sauce; serve with cheesecake.

Hot chocolate sauce
Combine ingredients in small saucepan; stir over low heat until smooth.

Serves 16

frozen peanut butter cheesecake

tiramisu cheesecake

¼ cup (20g) medium ground
  espresso coffee
1 cup (250ml) boiling water
2 tablespoons caster sugar
⅓ cup (80ml) marsala
250g savoiardi sponge
  finger biscuits
150g chocolate-coated coffee
  beans, chopped coarsely
Filling
2 teaspoons gelatine
2 tablespoons water
125g cream cheese, softened
¼ cup (40g) icing sugar
250g mascarpone
2 tablespoons marsala
300ml thickened cream,
  whipped

1 Grease 24cm round springform tin.
2 Combine coffee and the water in coffee plunger; stand 4 minutes before plunging. Combine coffee, sugar and marsala in medium heatproof bowl; cool 10 minutes.
3 Place ⅓ cup (80ml) coffee mixture in small saucepan; simmer, uncovered, until reduced to about 1 tablespoon. Cool.
4 Cut each biscuit into 7cm lengths; reserve end pieces. Dip flat side of biscuit lengths one at a time in remaining coffee mixture; arrange biscuits, round side out, around side of tin. Dip reserved biscuit ends in coffee mixture; place over base of tin.
5 Make filling by sprinkling gelatine over the water in small heatproof jug; stand jug in small saucepan of simmering water. Stir until gelatine dissolves. Cool 5 minutes.

6 Beat cheese and sifted sugar in medium bowl with electric mixer until smooth. Add mascarpone and marsala; beat until combined. Stir in gelatine mixture; fold in whipped cream.
7 Spread filling into tin. Drizzle reduced coffee mixture over cheesecake, pull skewer backwards and forwards several times for marbled effect. Refrigerate overnight.
8 Serve cheesecake topped with chocolate-coated coffee beans.

Serves 12

double-choc mousse cheesecake

125g plain chocolate biscuits
75g butter, melted
150g dark eating chocolate, melted
Filling
3 teaspoons gelatine
¼ cup (60ml) water
500g cream cheese, softened
½ cup (110g) caster sugar
2 eggs, separated
1 cup (250ml) cream
150g dark eating chocolate, melted
100g white eating chocolate, melted
2 tablespoons cream, extra

1 Line 22cm springform tin with plastic wrap (see page 353).
2 Process biscuits until fine. Add butter; process until combined. Press mixture over base of tin. Refrigerate 30 minutes.
3 Make filling by sprinkling gelatine over the water in small heatproof jug; stand jug in small saucepan of simmering water. Stir until gelatine dissolves; cool 5 minutes.
4 Beat cheese, sugar and egg yolks in medium bowl with electric mixer until smooth; beat in cream. Stir in dark chocolate and gelatine mixture.
5 Beat egg whites in small bowl with electric mixer until soft peaks form; fold into cheese mixture. Pour filling into tin.
6 Combine white chocolate and extra cream in small jug. Swirl white chocolate mixture through cheesecake mixture. Refrigerate overnight.

7 Spread dark chocolate over baking paper to a 20cm square. When set, break chocolate into small pieces.
8 Remove cheesecake from tin to serving plate. Press chocolate pieces around side of cheesecake.

Serves 12

triple-choc cheesecake cones

3 teaspoons gelatine
¼ cup (60ml) water
1 egg
500g cream cheese, softened
½ cup (110g) caster sugar
2 teaspoons vanilla extract
1¾ cups (430ml) cream
80g white eating chocolate, melted
80g milk eating chocolate
1 tablespoon Baileys Irish Cream
80g dark eating chocolate
1 tablespoon cocoa powder

1 Cut six 30cm squares from baking paper; fold squares in half diagonally. Place one triangle on bench with centre point towards you; curl one point towards you, turning it under where it meets the centre point. Hold these two points together with one hand then roll remaining point towards you to meet the other two, turning it under to form a cone. Staple or tape the cone securely to hold its shape; stand cone upright in a tall glass. Repeat with remaining triangles; place glasses on tray.
2 Sprinkle gelatine over the water in small heatproof jug; stand jug in small saucepan of simmering water. Stir until gelatine dissolves; cool 5 minutes.
3 Beat egg, cheese, sugar and extract in medium bowl with electric mixer until smooth; beat in cream. Stir in gelatine mixture.

4 Divide mixture into three bowls in 1-cup (250ml), 1½-cup (375ml) and 2-cup (500ml) quantities. Fold white chocolate into the 1-cup mixture; divide evenly among cones. Freeze 15 minutes or until layer is starting to set. Remove from freezer; scratch surface of cheesecake with fork.
5 Melt milk chocolate; fold into the 1½-cup mixture with Baileys. Divide evenly among cones. Freeze 15 minutes or until layer is just starting to set. Remove from freezer; scratch surface of cheesecake with fork.
6 Melt dark chocolate; fold into the 2-cup mixture with sifted cocoa. Divide evenly among cones. Cover cones loosely with plastic wrap; refrigerate overnight.
7 Place cones on serving plates; remove paper. Serve immediately, with fresh blueberries, if desired.

Serves 6

choc hazelnut éclairs

80g butter
1 cup (250ml) water
1 cup (150g) plain flour
4 eggs, beaten lightly
¼ cup (35g) roasted hazelnuts,
   chopped coarsely
Filling
⅔ cup (160ml) thickened cream
1½ tablespoons icing sugar
250g cream cheese, softened
2 tablespoons Frangelico
50g dark eating chocolate,
   chopped finely
Chocolate glaze
60g butter
125g dark eating chocolate,
   chopped coarsely

1 Preheat oven to 220°C/200°C fan-forced. Grease two oven trays.
2 Combine butter and the water in small saucepan; bring to a boil. Add flour; beat, over heat, with wooden spoon until mixture comes away from base and side of pan to form a smooth ball.
3 Transfer mixture to small bowl; gradually beat in egg with electric mixer until mixture becomes glossy.
4 Spoon choux pastry into piping bag fitted with 3cm plain tube. Pipe 6cm lengths of mixture, 3cm apart, onto trays; bake 10 minutes. Reduce oven temperature to 180°C/160°C fan-forced; bake about 10 minutes or until éclairs are browned lightly. Split éclairs in half, remove any soft centres; return to trays. Bake about 5 minutes or until éclairs are dried out. Cool.

5 Make filling by beating cream and sifted icing sugar in small bowl with electric mixer until soft peaks form. Beat cheese and Frangelico in small bowl with electric mixer until smooth. Fold in chocolate, then cream. Refrigerate.
6 Make chocolate glaze.
7 Spoon filling into 12 éclair halves. Dip remaining halves into chocolate glaze; sprinkle with nuts. When glaze is firm, sandwich éclair halves together.

Chocolate glaze
Combine butter and chocolate in small saucepan; stir over low heat until smooth.

Makes 12

mocha crème brûlée cheesecakes

75g butter, chopped
50g dark eating chocolate, chopped
½ cup (110g) caster sugar
¼ cup (60ml) water
1 tablespoon Kahlua
½ cup (75g) plain flour
1 tablespoon cocoa powder
1 egg yolk
1 tablespoon caster sugar, extra

Crème brûlée filling
2 teaspoons gelatine
2 tablespoons water
2 tablespoons Kahlua
2 teaspoons instant coffee granules
500g cream cheese, softened
½ cup (110g) caster sugar
2 teaspoons vanilla extract
1 cup (250ml) cream

1 Preheat oven to 160°C/140°C fan-forced. Grease 20cm x 30cm lamington pan; line base and sides with baking paper, extending paper 5cm over long sides.
2 Combine butter, chocolate, sugar, the water and liqueur in small saucepan. Stir over low heat until smooth.
3 Transfer mixture to small bowl; cool 10 minutes. Whisk in sifted flour and cocoa, then egg yolk. Pour mixture into pan; bake about 20 minutes. Cool in pan.
4 Cut six rounds from cake large enough to cover bases of six ¾ cup (180ml) heatproof dishes.
5 Make crème brûlée filling by sprinkling gelatine over the water and liqueur in small heatproof jug; stand jug in small saucepan of simmering water. Stir until gelatine dissolves; add coffee, stir until dissolved. Cool 5 minutes.

6 Beat cheese, sugar and extract in medium bowl with electric mixer until smooth; beat in cream. Add coffee mixture; beat until smooth. Divide filling among dishes; refrigerate 3 hours or overnight.
7 Preheat grill on highest setting. Sprinkle extra sugar evenly over cheesecakes. Using finger, press gently onto surface of cheesecakes; place under grill until tops have caramelised.

Serves 6

125g butter, softened
1 cup (220g) caster sugar
2 eggs
1 cup (150g) roasted pistachios, chopped coarsely
2 cups (300g) self-raising flour
⅔ cup (160ml) milk
1 tablespoon icing sugar
¼ teaspoon ground cardamom
Filling
2 teaspoons gelatine
2 tablespoons water
125g cream cheese, softened
¾ cup (165g) caster sugar
2 tablespoons lemon juice
1 teaspoon rose water
pink food colouring
1 cup (250g) mascarpone
300ml thickened cream, whipped

1 Preheat oven to 180°C/160°C fan-forced. Grease 22cm springform tin; line base with baking paper.
2 Beat butter and sugar in small bowl with electric mixer until light and fluffy. Beat in eggs, one at a time, until combined; transfer mixture to large bowl.
3 Stir in nuts, sifted flour and milk in two batches. Spread mixture in tin; bake about 50 minutes. Stand cake 5 minutes; turn onto wire rack to cool.
4 Make filling by sprinkling gelatine over the water in small heatproof jug; stand jug in small saucepan of simmering water. Stir until gelatine dissolves. Cool 5 minutes.
5 Beat cheese, sugar, juice and rose water in medium bowl with electric mixer until smooth. Beat in enough colouring to tint mixture pale pink. Add mascarpone; beat until combined. Stir in gelatine mixture; fold in cream.

6 Split cake in half; return bottom layer to tin. Spread filling over cake; refrigerate 30 minutes. Top with remaining cake; refrigerate 3 hours.
7 Serve cheesecake dusted with sifted icing sugar and cardamom.

Serves 8

rose water and pistachio cheesecake

mint chocolate truffle cheesecakes

You need an 80cm length of 50mm diameter PVC pipe, cut into 10cm lengths; ask the hardware store to do this for you, or use a hacksaw. This recipe will also fit into six 10cm round springform tins or a 24cm springform tin.

125g plain chocolate biscuits
35g Peppermint Crisp
   chocolate bar
75g butter, melted
Filling
2 teaspoons gelatine
2 tablespoons water
500g cream cheese, softened
½ cup (110g) caster sugar
¼ cup (60ml) crème de menthe
   liqueur
1½ cups (375ml) thickened
   cream, whipped
Truffles
2 tablespoons thickened cream
100g dark eating chocolate,
   chopped coarsely
2 x 35g Peppermint Crisp
   chocolate bars, chopped finely

1 Make truffles.
2 Stand eight 10cm lengths of cleaned PVC pipe on tray; line each pipe with baking paper.
3 Process biscuits and Peppermint Crisp until fine. Add butter; process until combined. Divide mixture among pipes; using end of wooden spoon, press mixture down evenly. Refrigerate 30 minutes.
4 Make filling by sprinkling gelatine over the water in small heatproof jug; stand jug in small saucepan of simmering water. Stir until gelatine dissolves. Cool 5 minutes.
5 Beat cream cheese and sugar in medium bowl with electric mixer until smooth. Stir in gelatine mixture and liqueur; fold in cream. Divide filling among pipes; refrigerate overnight.
6 Remove pipes and paper from cheesecakes. Serve topped with truffles and mint leaves, if desired.

Truffles
Combine cream and dark chocolate in small saucepan; stir over low heat until smooth. Transfer mixture to small bowl, cover; refrigerate 3 hours. Roll ½ teaspoonfuls of mixture into balls; place on tray. Roll balls in Peppermint Crisp; return to tray. Refrigerate truffles until firm.

Makes 8

ginger cake with lime

250g butter, chopped
½ cup (110g) firmly packed
    dark brown sugar
⅔ cup (230g) golden syrup
12cm piece fresh ginger (60g),
    grated
¾ cup (180ml) cream
2 eggs
1 cup (150g) plain flour
1 cup (150g) self-raising flour
½ teaspoon bicarbonate of soda
Filling
½ teaspoon gelatine
1 tablespoon lime juice
125g cream cheese, softened
1 teaspoon finely grated
    lime rind
1 tablespoon caster sugar
¼ cup (60ml) cream
Lime syrup
½ cup (110g) caster sugar
½ cup (125ml) lime juice
½ cup (125ml) water
2 teaspoons finely grated
    lime rind

1 Preheat oven to 180°C/160°C
fan-forced. Grease deep 22cm-
round cake pan; line base and
side with baking paper.
2 Combine butter, sugar, golden
syrup and ginger in medium
saucepan; stir over low heat
until sugar dissolves. Remove
from heat. Whisk in cream, then
eggs and sifted flours and soda.
3 Pour mixture into pan; bake
about 1 hour. Stand cake in pan
10 minutes; turn cake onto wire
rack to cool.
4 Make filling by sprinkling
gelatine over juice in small
heatproof jug; stand jug in small
saucepan of simmering water.
Stir until gelatine dissolves. Cool
5 minutes. Beat cheese, rind,
sugar and cream in small bowl
with electric mixer until smooth.
Stir in gelatine mixture.

5 Split cake horizontally a
quarter of the way from the
top; set aside. Place large
piece of cake on serving plate.
Using small teaspoon or melon
baller, scoop 18 holes (at equal
distances apart and not through
to bottom) out of cake. Pour
filling mixture into holes;
replace top of cake. Cover;
refrigerate overnight.
6 Make lime syrup.
7 Serve cake drizzled with
lime syrup.

Lime syrup
Combine sugar, juice and the
water in small saucepan; stir, over
heat, until sugar dissolves. Boil,
uncovered, 10 minutes or until
syrup thickens slightly. Remove
from heat; stir in rind. Cool.

Serves 12

250g plain sweet biscuits
125g butter, melted
Filling
1 teaspoon gelatine
1 tablespoon water
250g cream cheese, softened
2 teaspoons finely grated
   lemon rind
395g can sweetened
   condensed milk
⅓ cup (80ml) lemon juice
Lemon rind syrup
⅓ cup (75g) caster sugar
⅓ cup (80ml) water
2 tablespoons shredded
   lemon rind

1 Process biscuits until fine. Add butter, process until combined. Press mixture over base and side of 20cm springform tin. Refrigerate 30 minutes.
2 Make filling by sprinkling gelatine over the water in small heatproof jug; stand jug in small saucepan of simmering water. Stir until gelatine dissolves; cool 5 minutes.
3 Beat cheese and rind in small bowl with electric mixer until smooth. Add condensed milk and juice; beat until smooth. Stir in gelatine mixture.
4 Pour filling into tin; refrigerate cheesecake overnight.
5 Make lemon rind syrup; serve with cheesecake.

Lemon rind syrup
Stir sugar and the water in small saucepan, over low heat, until sugar is dissolved; simmer 2 minutes. Add rind, simmer until syrup is thickened slightly; cool.

Serves 8

classic lemon cheesecake

185g ginger nut biscuits
60g butter, melted
Filling
3 teaspoons gelatine
¼ cup (60ml) water
500g cream cheese, softened
⅓ cup (55g) firmly packed
  brown sugar
300ml cream
½ cup (125ml) maple syrup
Topping
1¼ cups (175g) pecans,
  chopped coarsely
2 tablespoons maple syrup

1 Grease deep 19cm square cake pan; line base and sides with two sheets baking paper, extending paper 5cm above edges of pan.

2 Process biscuits until fine. Add butter; process until combined. Press mixture over base of pan; refrigerate 30 minutes.

3 Make filling by sprinkling gelatine over the water in small heatproof jug; stand jug in small saucepan of simmering water. Stir until gelatine dissolves. Cool 5 minutes.

4 Beat cheese and sugar in medium bowl with electric mixer until smooth; beat in cream and maple syrup. Stir in gelatine mixture.

5 Pour filling mixture into pan; refrigerate overnight.

6 Make topping.

7 Serve cheesecake sprinkled with topping.

Topping
Preheat oven to 240°C/220°C fan-forced. Combine nuts and maple syrup in small bowl; spread mixture onto greased oven tray. Roast 10 minutes or until browned lightly; cool.

Serves 12

maple pecan cheesecake

malted milkshake cheesecakes

200g chocolate mudcake
90g Maltesers, crushed
⅓ cup (80ml) chocolate liqueur
Filling
3 teaspoons gelatine
¼ cup (60ml) water
500g cream cheese, softened
½ cup (110g) caster sugar
½ cup (60g) powdered malt
1 cup (250ml) thickened cream
2 eggs, separated
100g dark eating chocolate,
   melted
Topping
55g Maltesers

1 Cut mudcake into 1cm cubes; divide among eight 1 cup (250ml) glasses. Top with crushed Maltesers and liqueur.
2 Make filling by sprinkling gelatine over the water in small heatproof jug; stand jug in small saucepan of simmering water. Stir until gelatine dissolves. Cool 5 minutes.
3 Beat cheese, sugar and malt in medium bowl with electric mixer until smooth; beat in cream and egg yolks. Stir in gelatine mixture, then chocolate.
4 Beat egg whites in small bowl with electric mixer until firm peaks form; fold into chocolate mixture.
5 Divide filling among glasses; refrigerate overnight.
6 Serve cheesecake topped with whole Maltesers.

Serves 8

berry nougat cheesecake

125g butternut snap biscuits
60g butter, melted
100g almond nougat,
    chopped finely
300g frozen raspberries
Filling
2 teaspoons gelatine
2 tablespoons water
375g cream cheese, softened
¼ cup (55g) caster sugar
2 teaspoons lemon juice
300ml cream

1 Line 22cm springform tin with plastic wrap (see page 353).
2 Process biscuits until fine. Add butter; process until combined. Stir in nougat. Press mixture over base of tin. Refrigerate 30 minutes.
3 Make filling by sprinkling gelatine over the water in small heatproof jug; stand jug in small saucepan of simmering water. Stir until gelatine dissolves. Cool 5 minutes.
4 Beat cheese, sugar and juice in small bowl with electric mixer until smooth; beat in cream. Stir in gelatine mixture.
5 Sprinkle half the raspberries over base; spread with filling. Refrigerate overnight.
6 Blend or process remaining raspberries; strain. Serve cheesecake with berry coulis.

Serves 10

250g butternut snap biscuits
50g butter, melted
Filling
1 teaspoon gelatine
2 tablespoons lime juice
¼ cup (65g) grated palm sugar
250g cream cheese, softened
2 teaspoons finely grated
  lime rind
1 cup (250ml) cream
Palm sugar syrup
1 lime
½ cup (125ml) water
⅓ cup (90g) grated palm sugar

1 Grease 12-hole (¼ cup/60ml) mini cheesecake pan with removable bases.
2 Process biscuits until fine. Add butter; process until combined. Divide mixture among holes; press firmly. Refrigerate 30 minutes.
3 Make filling by sprinkling gelatine over juice in small heatproof jug; stand jug in small saucepan of simmering water. Stir until gelatine dissolves. Cool 5 minutes. Stir in sugar.
4 Beat cheese and rind in small bowl with electric mixer until smooth; beat in cream. Stir in gelatine mixture. Divide filling mixture among holes; refrigerate overnight.
5 Make palm sugar syrup.
6 Serve cheesecakes with palm sugar syrup.

Palm sugar syrup
Remove rind from lime; cut into thin strips. Stir the water and sugar in small saucepan over low heat until sugar dissolves. Boil, uncovered, without stirring, about 5 minutes or until syrup thickens slightly. Remove from heat; add rind. Cool.

Serves 12

palm sugar and lime cheesecakes

vanilla cheesecake slice

2 sheets ready-rolled puff pastry
Custard
½ cup (110g) caster sugar
⅓ cup (50g) cornflour
¼ cup (30g) custard powder
2 cups (500ml) milk
40g butter, chopped
2 egg yolks
2 teaspoons vanilla extract
Filling
1½ teaspoons gelatine
1 tablespoon water
250g cream cheese, softened
⅓ cup (75g) caster sugar
¾ cup (180ml) cream
Passionfruit icing
1½ cups (240g) icing sugar
1 teaspoon soft butter
2 tablespoons passionfruit pulp

1 Preheat oven to 240°C/220°C fan-forced. Grease 23cm square cake pan; line base and sides with foil, extending foil 5cm above edges of pan.
2 Place pastry sheets on greased oven trays; prick all over with a fork. Bake about 10 minutes or until browned well; cool. Flatten pastry sheets; place one sheet into pan.
3 Make custard by blending sugar, cornflour and custard powder in medium saucepan with milk. Stir over heat until mixture boils and thickens. Remove from heat, stir in butter, egg yolks and extract. Pour hot custard over pastry. Cool 15 minutes.
4 Make filling by sprinkling gelatine over the water in small heatproof jug; stand jug in small saucepan of simmering water. Stir until gelatine dissolves. Cool 5 minutes.

5 Beat cheese, sugar and cream in small bowl with electric mixer until smooth. Stir in gelatine mixture; spread over custard in pan, top with remaining pastry, flat side up, press down gently. Refrigerate 4 hours.
6 Make passionfruit icing.
7 Spread pastry with passionfruit icing. Cut slice when icing is set.

Passionfruit icing
Sift icing sugar into small heatproof bowl; stir in butter and passionfruit. Place bowl over saucepan of hot water; stir until icing is spreadable.

Serves 12

berry pavlova cheesecakes

2 egg whites
⅓ cup (80ml) boiling water
½ teaspoon cream of tartar
1½ cups (330g) caster sugar
1 cup (150g) frozen
    mixed berries

Filling

250g cream cheese
250g cottage cheese
1 cup (160g) icing sugar
1 teaspoon vanilla extract
⅔ cup (190g) yogurt
1 cup (150g) frozen
    mixed berries

1 Preheat oven to 150°C/130°C fan-forced. Grease and line two oven trays with baking paper; mark three 8cm-diameter circles on each tray.

2 Combine egg whites, the water, cream of tartar and sugar in medium, deep, heatproof bowl. Stand bowl over medium saucepan of barely simmering water – water should not touch bottom of bowl. Beat with electric mixer about 12 minutes or until mixture is stiff and glossy.

3 Divide mixture among circles; shape into nests. Bake 1 hour; cool in oven with door ajar.

4 Make filling by beating cheeses, sifted icing sugar and extract in medium bowl with electric mixer until combined; fold in yogurt and berries. Refrigerate 2 hours.

5 Gently press top of each meringue nest to make a small hollow. Divide filling among meringues; top with berries. Serve dusted with a little sifted icing sugar, if desired.

Makes 6

frozen citrus yogurt cheesecakes

500g cream cheese, softened
1 cup (220g) caster sugar
3 cups (800g) vanilla yogurt
1 tablespoon finely grated
 lemon rind
1 tablespoon finely grated
 lime rind
½ cup (120ml) orange juice
⅓ cup (80ml) lemon juice
2 tablespoons lime juice
orange food colouring
⅓ cup (25g) shredded coconut,
 toasted

1 Place a collar of foil around six ¾-cup (180ml) dishes; secure with string.
2 Beat cheese and sugar in medium bowl with electric mixer until smooth. Gradually add yogurt; beat until smooth. Stir in rinds, juices and enough food colouring to tint mixture pale orange.
3 Divide mixture among dishes. Cover loosely with plastic wrap; freeze overnight.
4 Remove cheesecakes from freezer; stand 5 minutes. Remove collars; press coconut around sides of cheesecakes. Freeze 5 minutes before serving.

Serves 6

cookies

There have never been cookies quite like these before. Fantastic and imaginative, these ideas will excite the baker as much as every volunteer taste-tester. The sensationally original creations you'll find here are so versatile they're the perfect gift for the person who has everything as well as being a child's birthday party-stopper. So, who did steal the cookie from the cookie jar?

malted milk number cookies

125g butter, softened
½ cup (110g) caster sugar
1 egg
¼ cup (90g) golden syrup
¼ cup (30g) malted milk powder
2½ cups (375g) plain flour
½ teaspoon bicarbonate of soda
1½ teaspoons cream of tartar
Green icing
1 egg white, beaten lightly
1½ cups (240g) icing sugar
2 teaspoons plain flour
2 teaspoons lemon juice,
   approximately
green food colouring

1 Beat butter, sugar and egg in small bowl with electric mixer until combined. Stir in golden syrup and sifted dry ingredients, in two batches.
2 Knead dough on floured surface until smooth; roll dough between sheets of baking paper until 5mm thick. Refrigerate 30 minutes.
3 Preheat oven to 150°C/130°C fan-forced. Grease oven trays; line with baking paper.
4 Using 6cm number cutters (see page 359), cut 45 numbers from dough; place about 3cm apart on oven trays. Bake about 15 minutes. Cool on trays.
5 Make green icing. Spread cookie numbers with icing; set at room temperature.

Green icing
Place egg white in small bowl, stir in half the sifted icing sugar, then remaining sifted icing sugar, flour and enough juice to make a thick, spreadable icing. Tint icing green.

Makes 45

double-choc freckle cookies

125g butter, softened
¾ cup (165g) firmly packed
  brown sugar
1 egg
1½ cups (225g) plain flour
¼ cup (35g) self-raising flour
¼ cup (35g) cocoa powder
200g dark eating chocolate,
  melted
⅓ cup (85g) hundreds
  and thousands

1 Beat butter, sugar and egg in small bowl with electric mixer until combined. Stir in sifted dry ingredients, in two batches.

2 Knead dough on floured surface until smooth; roll dough between sheets of baking paper until 5mm thick. Cover; refrigerate 30 minutes.

3 Preheat oven to 180°C/160°C fan-forced. Grease oven trays; line with baking paper.

4 Using 3cm, 5cm and 6.5cm round cutters, cut 14 rounds from dough using each cutter. Place 3cm rounds on one oven tray; place remainder on other oven trays.

5 Bake small cookies about 10 minutes; bake larger cookies about 12 minutes. Cool on wire racks.

6 Spread tops of cookies with chocolate; sprinkle with hundreds and thousands. Set at room temperature.

Makes 42

125g butter, softened
½ cup (110g) caster sugar
1 egg
¼ cup (60ml) golden syrup
2½ cups (375g) plain flour
½ teaspoon bicarbonate of soda
1½ teaspoons cream of tartar
1 teaspoon ground ginger
1 teaspoon ground mixed spice
½ teaspoon ground clove
Pink icing
1 egg white, beaten lightly
1½ cups (240g) icing sugar
2 teaspoons plain flour
2 teaspoons lemon juice,
   approximately
pink food colouring

1 Beat butter, sugar and egg in medium bowl with electric mixer until combined. Stir in syrup and sifted dry ingredients, in two batches.
2 Knead dough on floured surface until smooth; roll dough between sheets of baking paper until 5mm thick. Cover; refrigerate 30 minutes.
3 Preheat oven to 150°C/130°C fan-forced. Grease oven trays; line with baking paper.
4 Using 9cm cross cutter and 7.5cm zero cutter (see page 359), cut shapes from dough. Place about 3cm apart on oven trays.
5 Bake shapes about 15 minutes. Cool on trays.
6 Make pink icing. Spread jumbles with pink icing; set at room temperature

Pink icing
Place egg white in small bowl, stir in half the sifted icing sugar; add remaining sifted icing sugar, flour and enough juice to make a thick spreadable icing. Tint icing pink.

Makes 32

jumble bumbles

100g butter, softened
½ cup (150g) caster sugar
1 egg
2 cups (300g) plain flour
1 tablespoon cocoa powder
100g dark eating chocolate,
  melted

Macaroon filling

1 egg white
¼ cup (55g) caster sugar
½ teaspoon vanilla extract
¾ cup (60g) desiccated coconut
1 teaspoon plain flour
2 tablespoons finely chopped
  red glacé cherries

1 Make macaroon filling.
2 Beat butter, sugar and egg in small bowl with electric mixer until light and fluffy; stir in sifted dry ingredients, in two batches. Stir in chocolate.
3 Knead dough on floured surface until smooth. Roll dough between sheets of baking paper until 7mm thick.
4 Preheat oven to 180°C/160°C fan-forced. Grease oven trays; line with baking paper.
5 Using 8cm heart-shaped cutter (see page 359), cut hearts from dough. Place, about 2cm apart, on oven trays. Using 4cm heart-shaped cutter, cut out centres from hearts.
6 Bake cookies about 7 minutes; remove from oven. Reduce oven temperature to 150°C/130°C fan-forced.

7 Divide macaroon mixture among centres of cookies; smooth surface. Cover with foil (like a tent so foil does not touch surface of macaroon). Bake about 15 minutes or until macaroon is firm. Cool on trays 5 minutes; transfer to wire racks to cool.

Macaroon filling
Beat egg white in small bowl with electric mixer until soft peaks form. Gradually add sugar 1 tablespoon at a time, beating until dissolved between additions. Fold in extract, coconut, flour and cherries.

Makes 22

choc-cherry macaroon heart cookies

choc-cherry bliss bombs

1⅓ cups (200g) milk chocolate
    Melts
60g butter
¼ cup (60ml) vegetable oil
⅓ cup (75g) caster sugar
2 eggs
1 cup (150g) self-raising flour
1 cup (150g) plain flour
3 x 55g Cherry Ripe bars,
    chopped finely
¼ cup (20g) desiccated coconut

1 Stir chocolate, butter, oil and sugar in medium saucepan over low heat until smooth. Cool 15 minutes.
2 Preheat oven to 180°C/160°C fan-forced. Grease oven trays; line with baking paper.
3 Stir eggs and flours into chocolate mixture; stir in Cherry Ripe.
4 Roll level ½ teaspoons of mixture into balls; roll half the balls in coconut. Place about 2cm apart on oven trays.
5 Bake cookies about 10 minutes. Cool on trays.
6 Serve in paper cones (see page 358).

Makes 280

wedding cake cookies

⅓ cup (55g) dried mixed fruit
2 tablespoons brandy
125g butter, softened
1 teaspoon finely grated
  orange rind
⅓ cup (75g) caster sugar
1 tablespoon golden syrup
1 cup (150g) self-raising flour
⅔ cup (100g) plain flour
½ teaspoon mixed spice
Fondant icing
300g white prepared fondant,
  chopped coarsely
1 egg white
½ teaspoon lemon juice
Royal icing
1½ cups (240g) pure icing sugar
1 egg white

1 Process fruit and brandy
until smooth.
2 Beat butter, rind, sugar and
syrup in small bowl with electric
mixer until combined.
3 Stir in sifted dry ingredients
and fruit puree, in two batches.
4 Knead dough on floured
surface until smooth; roll dough
between sheets of baking
paper until 5mm thick. Cover;
refrigerate 30 minutes.
5 Preheat oven to 180°C/160°C
fan-forced. Grease oven trays;
line with baking paper.
6 Using 10.5cm wedding cake
cutter (see page 359), cut
12 shapes from dough. Place
about 5cm apart on oven trays.
Bake about 12 minutes. Cool
on wire racks.
7 Make fondant icing. Use a metal
spatula, dipped in hot water, to
spread icing quickly over cookies;
set at room temperature.
8 Make royal icing. Decorate
cookies with royal icing.

Fondant icing
Stir fondant in small heatproof
bowl over small saucepan of
simmering water until smooth.
Add egg white and juice; beat
until smooth.

Royal icing
Sift icing sugar through fine sieve.
Beat egg white until foamy in
small bowl with electric mixer;
beat in icing sugar, a tablespoon
at a time. Cover surface tightly
with plastic wrap.

Makes 12

christmas pudding cookies

1⅔ cups (250g) plain flour
⅓ cup (40g) almond meal
⅓ cup (75g) caster sugar
1 teaspoon mixed spice
1 teaspoon vanilla extract
125g cold butter, chopped
2 tablespoons water
700g rich dark fruit cake
⅓ cup (80ml) brandy
1 egg white
400g dark eating
   chocolate, melted
½ cup (75g) white chocolate
   Melts, melted
30 red glacé cherries

1 Process flour, meal, sugar, spice, extract and butter until crumbly. Add the water, process until ingredients come together.
2 Knead dough on floured surface until smooth; roll dough between sheets of baking paper until 5mm thick. Cover; refrigerate 30 minutes.
3 Preheat oven to 180°C/160°C fan-forced. Grease oven trays; line with baking paper.
4 Using 5.5cm round cutter (see page 359), cut 30 rounds from dough. Place about 3cm apart on oven trays. Bake about 10 minutes.
5 Meanwhile, crumble fruit cake into a medium bowl; add brandy. Press mixture firmly into round metal tablespoon measures. Brush partially baked cookies with egg white, top with cake domes; bake further 5 minutes. Cool on wire racks.
6 Place wire racks over oven tray, coat cookies with dark chocolate; set at room temperature.
7 Spoon white chocolate over cookies; top with cherries.

Makes 30

coconut fortune cookies

2 egg whites
⅓ cup (75g) caster sugar
⅓ cup (50g) plain flour
1 teaspoon coconut essence
30g butter, melted
½ teaspoon finely grated
   lime rind
2 tablespoons desiccated
   coconut
12 small paper messages

1 Preheat oven to 160°C/140°C fan-forced. Grease oven tray; line with baking paper. Mark two 9cm circles on paper.
2 Beat egg whites in small bowl with electric mixer until soft peaks form; gradually beat in sugar, beating until dissolved between additions.
3 Fold in sifted flour, essence, butter and rind. Drop one level tablespoon of mixture into centre of each circle on oven tray, spread evenly to cover circle completely; sprinkle with a little coconut. Bake about 5 minutes.
4 Working quickly, loosen cookies from tray, place message in the centre of cookies; fold in half then gently bend cookies over edge of a glass (see page 354). Cool 30 seconds. Transfer to wire rack to cool. Repeat with remaining cookie mixture and coconut.

Makes 12

⅔ cup (160ml) passionfruit pulp
¼ cup (55g) finely chopped
   glacé ginger
½ cup (55g) finely chopped
   glacé pineapple
½ cup (90g) finely chopped
   dried papaya
1 cup (75g) shredded coconut
1 cup (60g) coarsely crushed
   cornflakes
½ cup (70g) macadamia nuts,
   chopped finely
¾ cup (180ml) condensed milk
1 cup (150g) white chocolate
   Melts

1 Preheat oven to 180°C/160°C fan-forced. Grease oven trays; line with baking paper.

2 Strain passionfruit pulp; you need ⅓ cup (80ml) juice. Discard seeds.

3 Combine ginger, pineapple, papaya, coconut, cornflakes, nuts, milk and 2 tablespoons of the passionfruit juice in medium bowl.

4 Drop rounded tablespoonfuls of mixture about 5cm apart onto oven trays; press down slightly. Bake about 12 minutes. Cool on trays.

5 Combine chocolate with remaining passionfruit juice in small heatproof bowl; stir over small saucepan of simmering water until smooth. Spread chocolate over flat side of each florentine; mark with a fork. Set at room temperature.

Makes 25

tropical florentine cookies

rhubarb custard melting moments

You need to cook 1 large stem chopped rhubarb with about 1 tablespoon sugar (or to taste) and 1 tablespoon water over low heat, until rhubarb is pulpy. Drain, cool.

250g butter, softened
½ teaspoon vanilla extract
½ cup (80g) icing sugar
1 cup (125g) custard powder
1 cup (150g) plain flour
1 tablespoon icing sugar, extra
Rhubarb custard
1 tablespoon custard powder
1 tablespoon caster sugar
½ cup (125ml) milk
⅓ cup stewed rhubarb

1 Preheat oven to 160°C/140°C fan-forced. Grease oven trays; line with baking paper.
2 Make rhubarb custard.
3 Beat butter, extract and sifted icing sugar in small bowl with electric mixer until light and fluffy.
4 Stir in sifted custard powder and flour in two batches.
5 With floured hands, roll rounded teaspoons of mixture into balls. Place about 5cm apart on oven trays; flatten slightly with a floured fork.
6 Bake about 15 minutes. Stand 5 minutes; cool on wire racks.
7 Sandwich biscuits with a little rhubarb custard.

Rhubarb custard
Blend custard powder and sugar with milk in small saucepan; stir over heat until mixture boils and thickens. Remove from heat, stir in rhubarb. Cover surface of custard with plastic wrap; refrigerate until cold.

Makes 25

hot cross bun cookies

125g butter, softened
⅔ cup (150g) caster sugar
1 egg
¼ cup (40g) finely chopped
    mixed peel
½ cup (80g) dried currants
2 cups (300g) self-raising flour
1 teaspoon mixed spice
2 teaspoons milk
2 tablespoons almond meal
100g marzipan
2 tablespoons apricot jam,
    warmed, strained

1 Preheat oven to 160°C/140°C fan-forced. Grease oven trays, line with baking paper.
2 Beat butter, sugar and egg in small bowl with electric mixer until light and fluffy. Stir in peel, currants, sifted flour and spice, and milk in two batches.
3 Roll rounded teaspoons of mixture into balls; place about 5cm apart on oven trays.
4 Knead almond meal into marzipan. Roll marzipan into 5mm diameter sausages; cut into 4cm lengths.
5 Brush cookies with a little milk; place marzipan crosses on cookies, press down gently.
6 Bake about 15 minutes. Brush cookies with jam; cool on trays.

Makes 48

date and walnut scroll cookies

125g butter, softened
⅓ cup (75g) caster sugar
1 teaspoon ground cardamom
1 egg
1½ cups (225g) plain flour
1 cup (100g) walnuts, roasted,
   ground finely
2 cups (280g) dried dates,
   chopped coarsely
¼ cup (55g) caster sugar, extra
2 teaspoons finely grated
   lemon rind
⅓ cup (80ml) lemon juice
¼ teaspoon ground
   cardamom, extra
½ cup (125ml) water

1 Beat butter, sugar, cardamom and egg in small bowl with electric mixer until combined. Stir in sifted flour and walnuts.
2 Knead dough on floured surface until smooth; divide into two portions. Roll each portion between sheets of baking paper to 15cm x 30cm rectangles; refrigerate 20 minutes.
3 Meanwhile, stir dates, extra sugar, rind, juice, extra cardamom and the water in medium saucepan over heat, without boiling, until sugar is dissolved; bring to a boil. Reduce heat, simmer, uncovered, stirring occasionally, about 5 minutes or until mixture is thick and pulpy. Transfer to large bowl; refrigerate 10 minutes.

4 Spread filling evenly over the two rectangles, leaving 1cm border. Using paper as a guide, roll rectangles tightly from short side to enclose filling. Wrap rolls in baking paper; refrigerate 30 minutes.
5 Preheat oven to 190°C/170°C fan-forced. Grease oven trays; line with baking paper.
6 Trim edges of roll; cut each roll into 1cm slices. Place slices cut-side up on oven trays; bake about 20 minutes.

Makes 28

almond and plum crescents

1½ cups (225g) plain flour
½ cup (60g) almond meal
¼ cup (55g) caster sugar
2 teaspoons finely grated
   lemon rind
90g cream cheese, chopped
90g butter, chopped
2 tablespoons buttermilk
1 egg white
¼ cup (20g) flaked almonds,
   crushed lightly

Filling
⅓ cup (60g) finely chopped
   seeded prunes
¼ cup (80g) plum jam
¼ cup (55g) caster sugar
½ teaspoon ground cinnamon

1 Process flour, almond meal, sugar and rind until combined. Add cream cheese and butter, pulse until crumbly. Add buttermilk, process until ingredients come together.
2 Knead dough on floured surface until smooth. Divide dough in half. Roll each half between sheets of baking paper until large enough to be cut into 22cm rounds; cut dough using 22cm cake pan as a guide. Discard excess dough. Cover rounds; refrigerate 30 minutes.
3 Preheat oven to 180°C/160°C fan-forced. Grease oven trays; line with baking paper.
4 Make filling by combining ingredients in small bowl.
5 Cut each round into eight wedges, spread each wedge with a little filling mixture; roll from the wide end into a crescent shape. Place on oven trays, brush with egg white, sprinkle with flaked almonds. Bake about 25 minutes. Cool on trays.

Makes 16

apple crumble custard creams

1 medium fresh apple (150g),
   peeled, cored, chopped
   coarsely
2 teaspoons water
125g butter, softened
⅓ cup (75g) firmly packed
   brown sugar
2 tablespoons apple concentrate
1 cup (150g) self-raising flour
¾ cup (110g) plain flour
¼ cup (30g) oatbran
¼ cup (20g) desiccated coconut
1 teaspoon ground cinnamon
1 tablespoon icing sugar
Custard cream
1 tablespoon custard powder
1 tablespoon caster sugar
½ cup (125ml) milk
¼ teaspoon vanilla extract
125g cream cheese, softened

1 Stew apple with the water in small saucepan, covered, over medium heat until tender. Mash with a fork; cool.
2 Beat butter, sugar and concentrate in small bowl with electric mixer until combined.
3 Stir in sifted flours, oatbran, stewed apple, coconut and cinnamon, in two batches.
4 Knead dough on floured surface until smooth. Roll dough between sheets of baking paper until 3mm thick; refrigerate 30 minutes.
5 Preheat oven to 180°C/160°C fan-forced. Grease oven trays; line with baking paper.
6 Using 6.5cm apple cutter (see page 359), cut 40 shapes from dough. Place shapes about 3cm apart on oven trays. Bake about 12 minutes. Cool on wire racks.
7 Meanwhile, make custard cream.
8 Sandwich cookies with custard cream. Serve dusted with sifted icing sugar.

Custard cream
Blend custard powder and sugar with milk and extract in small saucepan; stir over heat until mixture boils and thickens. Remove from heat, cover surface with plastic wrap; cool. Beat cream cheese in small bowl with electric mixer until smooth. Add custard; beat until combined.

Makes 20

125g butter, softened
2 teaspoons finely grated
    lemon rind
½ teaspoon almond essence
½ cup (110g) caster sugar
1 egg
1⅔ cups (250g) plain flour
1 egg white
hundreds and thousands
12 paddle pop sticks
180g individually wrapped
    sugar-free fruit drops

1 Beat butter, rind, essence, sugar and egg in small bowl with electric mixer until combined. Stir in sifted flour, in two batches.
2 Knead dough on floured surface until smooth; roll dough between sheets of baking paper until 5mm thick. Cover; refrigerate 30 minutes.
3 Meanwhile, using rolling pin, gently tap wrapped lollies to crush slightly. Unwrap lollies; separate by colour into small bowls.
4 Preheat oven to 180°C/160°C fan-forced. Grease oven trays; line with baking paper.
5 Using 10.5cm round cutter (see page 359), cut 12 rounds from dough. Place about 5cm apart on oven trays.

6 Place 2.5cm, 5cm and 7.5cm cutters starting from the centre of each 10.5cm round. Remove dough between 5cm and 7.5cm cutters; remove dough from centre of 2.5cm cutter (see page 354). Brush half the remaining dough with egg white, sprinkle with hundreds and thousands. Slide one paddle pop stick under each cookie (see page 354).
7 Bake about 10 minutes. Remove trays from oven, fill gaps with crushed lollies; bake further 5 minutes. Cool on trays.

Makes 12

stained-glass lollypop cookies

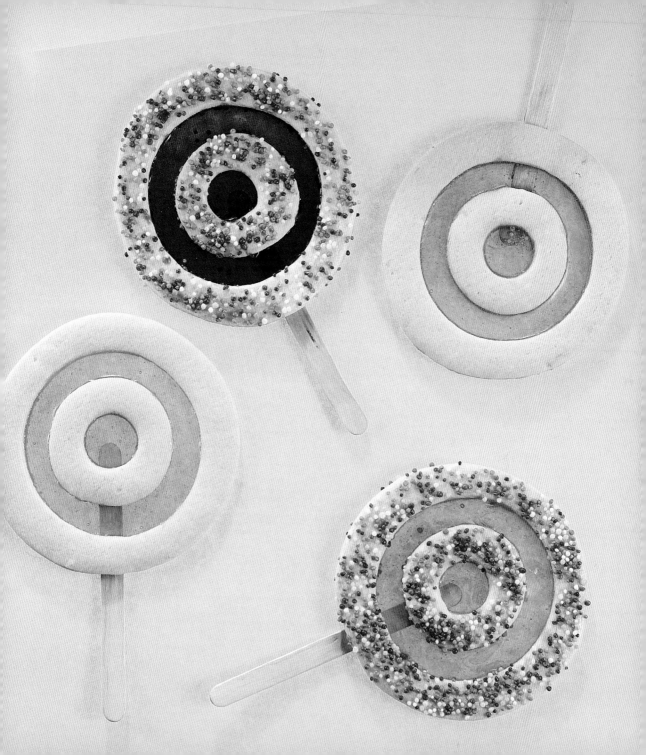

dancing shoe cookies

125g butter, softened
¾ cup (165g) firmly packed
  brown sugar
1 egg
1½ cups (225g) plain flour
¼ cup (35g) self-raising flour
¼ cup (25g) cocoa powder
100g dark eating chocolate,
  melted
silver cachous
Coloured sugar
⅔ cup (150g) caster sugar
pink, yellow, green and purple
  food colouring

1 Beat butter, sugar and egg in small bowl with electric mixer until combined. Stir in sifted flours and cocoa in two batches.
2 Knead dough on floured surface until smooth; roll dough between sheets of baking paper until 5mm thick. Cover; refrigerate 30 minutes.
3 Preheat oven to 180°C/160°C fan-forced. Grease oven trays; line with baking paper.
4 Using a 8.5cm shoe-shaped cutter, cut 25 shapes from dough. Place about 3cm apart on trays. Bake about 12 minutes. Cool on trays.
5 Make coloured sugar.
6 Spread cookies with chocolate. Sprinkle shoes with coloured sugar; decorate with cachous.

Coloured sugar
Divide sugar among four small plastic bags. Add different colouring to each bag to tint sugar. Rub colouring into sugar until combined.

Makes 25

ice-cream cone cookies

2 egg whites
⅓ cup (75g) caster sugar
⅓ cup (50g) plain flour
30g butter, melted
½ teaspoon vanilla extract
2 teaspoons cocoa powder
ice-cream

1 Preheat oven to 180°C/160°C fan-forced. Grease oven tray; line with baking paper. Mark a 10cm circle on paper.
2 Beat egg whites in small bowl with electric mixer until soft peaks form; gradually beat in sugar, beating until dissolved between additions. Stir in sifted flour, butter and extract.
3 Place ¼ cup of the mixture in small bowl, stir in sifted cocoa; spoon into a piping bag fitted with a small plain tube.
4 Place a level tablespoon of remaining mixture in centre of each circle on tray, spread evenly to fill circles. Pipe chocolate stripes across circles (see page 355).
5 Bake about 5 minutes. Working quickly, lift cookies from tray, shape into cones (see page 355). Cool on wire racks. Repeat with remaining cookie mixture.
6 Just before serving, fill cookie cones with ice-cream.

Makes 10

125g butter, softened

2 teaspoons finely grated
orange rind

1 cup (220g) firmly packed
brown sugar

1⅓ cups (200g) wholemeal
self-raising flour

1 cup (100g) walnuts, roasted,
chopped coarsely

⅔ cup (100g) raisins, halved

2 teaspoons dried rosemary

⅓ cup (80ml) orange juice

⅔ cup (50g) desiccated coconut

⅔ cup (60g) rolled oats

1 Preheat oven to 180°C/160°C fan-forced. Grease oven trays; line with baking paper.

2 Beat butter, rind and sugar in small bowl with electric mixer until combined. Transfer to medium bowl; stir in flour then remaining ingredients.

3 Roll rounded tablespoons of mixture into balls, place about 5cm apart on oven trays; flatten slightly. Bake about 15 minutes. Cool on trays.

Makes 28

wholemeal rosemary butter cookies

decadent mocha fingers

1 teaspoon instant
  coffee granules
2 teaspoons boiling water
125g butter, softened
¾ cup (165g) firmly packed
  brown sugar
1 egg
1½ cups (225g) plain flour
¼ cup (35g) self-raising flour
¼ cup (25g) cocoa powder
75 roasted coffee beans
Mocha custard
2 tablespoons custard powder
2 tablespoons caster sugar
60g dark eating chocolate,
  chopped roughly
1 cup (250ml) milk
1 tablespoon coffee liqueur

1 Blend coffee with the water. Beat butter, sugar and egg in small bowl with electric mixer until combined. Stir in coffee mixture, sifted flours and cocoa, in two batches.

2 Knead dough on floured surface until smooth; roll dough between sheets of baking paper until 4mm thick. Cover; refrigerate 30 minutes.

3 Preheat oven to 180°C/160°C fan-forced. Grease oven trays; line with baking paper.

4 Make mocha custard.

5 Using 8.5cm square cutter (see page 359), cut out 25 shapes from dough. Halve squares to make 50 rectangles; place on oven trays. Press three coffee beans on half of the rectangles.

6 Bake about 12 minutes. Cool on wire racks.

7 Spread mocha custard over plain cookies; top with coffee-bean topped cookies.

Mocha custard
Blend custard powder, sugar and chocolate with milk in small saucepan; stir over heat until mixture boils and thickens. Remove from heat, stir in liqueur. Cover surface with plastic wrap; refrigerate until cold.

Makes 25

double choc-chip chilli cookies

250g butter, softened
1 teaspoon vanilla extract
¾ cup (165g) caster sugar
¾ cup (165g) firmly packed
    brown sugar
1 egg
2 cups (300g) plain flour
¼ cup (25g) cocoa powder
1 teaspoon bicarbonate of soda
400g dark eating chocolate,
    chopped coarsely
Candied chillies
¼ cup (55g) caster sugar
¼ cup (60ml) water
3 fresh red thai chillies,
    chopped finely

1 Preheat oven to 180°C/160°C fan-forced. Grease oven trays; line with baking paper.
2 Make candied chillies.
3 Beat butter, extract, sugars and egg in small bowl with electric mixer until light and fluffy; transfer to large bowl.
4 Stir in sifted flour, cocoa and soda in two batches. Stir in chilli and chocolate.
5 Roll level tablespoons of dough into balls; place about 5cm apart on oven trays. Bake about 12 minutes. Cool on trays.

Candied chillies
Stir sugar and the water in small saucepan over heat until sugar dissolves. Add chilli, boil, 2 minutes; cool. Strain, discard syrup.

Makes 48

jammy flower cookies

125g butter, softened
½ teaspoon vanilla extract
½ cup (110g) caster sugar
1 cup (120g) almond meal
1 egg
1 cup (150g) plain flour
1 teaspoon finely grated
   lemon rind
⅓ cup (110g) raspberry jam
2 tablespoons apricot jam

1 Preheat oven to 180°C/160°C fan-forced. Grease oven trays; line with baking paper.
2 Beat butter, extract, sugar and almond meal in small bowl with electric mixer until light and fluffy. Add egg, beat until combined; stir in sifted flour.
3 Divide rind between both jams; mix well.
4 Roll level tablespoons of mixture into balls; place about 5cm apart on oven trays, flatten slightly. Using end of a wooden spoon, press a flower shape (about 1cm deep) into dough; fill each hole with a little jam, using apricot jam for centres of flowers.
5 Bake about 15 minutes. Cool on trays.

Makes 26

250g butter, softened
1 teaspoon vanilla extract
¾ cup (165g) caster sugar
¾ cup (165g) firmly packed
  brown sugar
1 egg
2 cups (300g) plain flour
¼ cup (25g) cocoa powder
1 teaspoon bicarbonate of soda
⅓ cup (45g) finely chopped
  roasted hazelnuts
⅔ cup (120g) coarsely chopped
  dark eating chocolate
⅔ cup (120g) coarsely chopped
  milk eating chocolate
⅔ cup (120g) coarsely chopped
  white eating chocolate

1 Preheat oven to 180°C/160°C fan-forced. Grease oven trays; line with baking paper.
2 Beat butter, extract, sugars and egg in small bowl with electric mixer until light and fluffy; transfer to large bowl.
3 Stir in sifted flour, cocoa and soda in two batches. Stir in nuts and chocolate.
4 Roll level tablespoons of dough into balls; place about 5cm apart on oven trays. Bake about 12 minutes. Cool on trays.

Makes 48

chocolate fudge brownie cookies

macadamia anzacs

125g butter, chopped
2 tablespoons golden syrup
½ teaspoon bicarbonate of soda
2 tablespoons boiling water
1 cup (90g) rolled oats
1 cup (150g) plain flour
1 cup (220g) firmly packed
   brown sugar
¾ cup (60g) desiccated coconut
½ cup (65g) finely chopped
   macadamia nuts
¼ cup (45g) finely chopped
   glacé ginger

1 Preheat oven to 180°C/160°C fan-forced. Grease oven trays; line with baking paper.
2 Combine butter and golden syrup in medium saucepan, stir over low heat until smooth.
3 Stir in combined soda and the water; stir in remaining ingredients.
4 Roll level tablespoons of mixture into balls. Place about 5cm apart on oven trays; flatten slightly. Bake about 15 minutes. Cool on trays.

Makes 32

jigsaw gingerbread people

125g butter, softened
½ cup (110g) firmly packed
   brown sugar
1 egg yolk
2½ cups (375g) plain flour
1 teaspoon bicarbonate of soda
3 teaspoons ground ginger
½ cup (175g) golden syrup
Lemon icing
1 egg white, beaten lightly
1½ cups (240g) icing sugar
2 teaspoons plain flour
2 teaspoons lemon juice,
   approximately
yellow food colouring

1 Preheat oven to 180°C/160°C fan-forced. Grease oven trays; line with baking paper.
2 Beat butter, sugar and egg yolk in small bowl with electric mixer until smooth; transfer to large bowl. Stir in sifted dry ingredients and syrup in two batches.
3 Knead dough on floured surface until smooth.
4 Divide dough in half; roll each half between sheets of baking paper until 5mm thick.
5 Place dough on oven tray. Using gingerbread people template, cut around shapes; remove excess dough (see page 355). Roll excess dough between sheets of baking paper until 5mm thick. Place dough on oven tray. Using heart template, cut around shape; remove excess dough (see page 355). Bake shapes about 15 minutes. Cool on trays.
6 Make lemon icing. Spread cookies with icing; set at room temperature.

Lemon icing
Place egg white in small bowl, stir in half the sifted icing sugar; stir in remaining sifted icing sugar, flour and enough juice to make a spreadable icing. Tint icing lemon.

Makes 24 pieces

mud cake cookie sandwiches

250g butter, softened
1½ cups (330g) firmly packed
   brown sugar
2 eggs
3 cups (450g) plain flour
½ cup (75g) self-raising flour
½ cup (50g) cocoa powder
2 tablespoons cocoa
   powder, extra

Chocolate mud cake
150g butter, chopped
100g dark eating chocolate,
   chopped coarsely
1 cup (220g) caster sugar
½ cup (125ml) water
2 tablespoons coffee liqueur
1 cup (150g) plain flour
2 tablespoons cocoa powder
2 egg yolks

Chocolate ganache
⅓ cup (80ml) cream
200g dark eating chocolate,
   chopped coarsely

1 Preheat oven to 170°C/150°C fan-forced. Grease two 20cm x 30cm lamington pans; line with a strip of baking paper, extending paper 2cm above edges of pans.
2 Make chocolate mud cake.
3 Make chocolate ganache.
4 Beat butter, sugar and eggs in small bowl with electric mixer until combined. Transfer mixture to large bowl; stir in sifted flours and cocoa, in two batches. Knead dough on floured surface until smooth; divide in half, roll each portion between sheets of baking paper until 5mm thick. Cover; refrigerate 30 minutes.
5 Preheat oven to 180°C/160°C fan-forced. Grease oven trays; line with baking paper.
6 Using 6.5cm round cutter (see page 359), cut 48 rounds from dough. Place about 3cm apart on oven trays. Bake about 12 minutes. Cool on wire racks.
7 Spread ganache onto underside of cookies; sandwich a mud cake round between two cookies.
8 Using heart template, dust cookies with extra cocoa.

Chocolate mud cake
Combine butter, chocolate, sugar, the water and liqueur in small saucepan. Stir over low heat until smooth. Place mixture in medium bowl; cool 10 minutes. Whisk in sifted flour and cocoa, then egg yolks. Divide mixture among pans. Bake about 25 minutes. Cool cakes in pans. Using 6.5cm round cutter (see page 359), cut 12 rounds from each cake.

Chocolate ganache
Bring cream to a boil in small saucepan; remove from heat. Add chocolate; stir until smooth. Refrigerate until spreadable.

Makes 24

choconut mint cookie stacks

You will need four 125g packets of After Dinner Mints for this recipe.

125g butter, softened
¾ cup (165g) firmly packed
  brown sugar
1 egg
1½ cups (225g) plain flour
¼ cup (35g) self-raising flour
2 tablespoons desiccated
  coconut
½ teaspoon coconut essence
2 tablespoons cocoa powder
40 square After Dinner Mints

1 Beat butter, sugar and egg in small bowl with electric mixer until combined. Stir in sifted flours in two batches. Place half the mixture into another small bowl; stir in coconut and essence. Stir sifted cocoa into the other bowl.

2 Knead each portion of dough on floured surface until smooth. Roll between sheets of baking paper until 3mm thick. Cover; refrigerate 30 minutes.

3 Preheat oven to 180°C/160°C fan-forced. Grease oven trays; line with baking paper.

4 Using 6cm square cutter (see page 359), cut 30 shapes from each portion of dough. Place about 3cm apart on oven trays.

5 Bake about 8 minutes. While cookies are still hot, sandwich three warm alternate-flavoured cookies with After Dinner Mints; press down gently. Cool on trays.

Makes 20

chocolate wheaten domino cookies

90g butter, softened
½ cup (110g) firmly packed
  brown sugar
1 egg
¼ cup (20g) desiccated
  coconut
¼ cup (25g) wheat germ
¾ cup (120g) wholemeal
  plain flour
⅓ cup (50g) white
  self-raising flour
¼ cup (45g) dark chocolate
  Bits, approximately
150g dark eating chocolate,
  melted

1 Beat butter and sugar in small bowl with electric mixer until smooth; add egg, beat until combined. Stir in coconut, wheat germ and sifted flours.

2 Roll dough between sheets of baking paper until 5mm thick. Cover; refrigerate 30 minutes.

3 Preheat oven to 180°C/160°C fan-forced. Grease oven trays; line with baking paper.

4 Using 9cm square cutter (see page 359), cut 14 squares from dough; cut each square in half to make 28 rectangles. Place about 3cm apart on oven trays. Using a knife, mark (do not cut through) each rectangle across the centre, to make two squares. Press chocolate Bits into each square to make dominoes.

5 Bake about 12 minutes. Cool on trays.

6 Spread bases of dominoes with melted chocolate; set at room temperature on baking-paper-lined oven trays.

Makes 28

christmas wreath cookies

Edible glitter is a non-metallic decoration available at cake decorating shops.

3 cups (450g) self-raising flour
125g butter
¼ cup (60ml) milk
⅔ cup (110g) caster sugar
1 teaspoon vanilla extract
2 eggs
silver edible glitter, to decorate
Lemon icing
3 cups (480g) icing sugar
2 tablespoons lemon juice, approximately

1 Preheat oven to 180°C/160°C fan-forced. Grease oven trays; line with baking paper.
2 Sift flour into medium bowl, rub in butter. Combine milk and sugar in small saucepan, stir over low heat until sugar is dissolved, add extract; cool 5 minutes. Stir combined warm milk mixture and egg into flour mixture.
3 Knead dough on floured surface until smooth.
4 Roll rounded teaspoons of dough into 13cm sausages. Twist two sausages together, form into circles; press edges together. Place about 3cm apart on oven trays.
5 Bake about 15 minutes. Cool on wire racks.
6 Meanwhile, make lemon icing. Drizzle wreaths with icing; set at room temperature. Sprinkle with edible glitter.

Lemon icing
Sift icing sugar into small heatproof bowl; stir in enough juice to make a firm paste. Stir over small saucepan of simmering water until pourable.

Makes 30

lemon grass, ginger and sesame bars

You will need eight 40g packets of original sesame snaps for this recipe.

125g butter, softened
⅔ cup (130g) firmly packed grated palm sugar
½ teaspoon ground cardamom
½ teaspoon ground cinnamon
pinch ground nutmeg
pinch ground clove
2 egg yolks
1½ cups (225g) plain flour
10cm stick (20g) fresh lemon grass, chopped finely
2 tablespoons finely chopped glacé ginger
32 sesame snaps

1 Beat butter, sugar, spices and egg yolks in small bowl with electric mixer until smooth. Stir in sifted flour, lemon grass and ginger.
2 Knead dough on floured surface until smooth. Roll dough between sheets of baking paper until 5mm thick; refrigerate 30 minutes.
3 Preheat oven to 160°C/140°C fan-forced. Grease oven trays; line with baking paper.
4 Using 9cm square cutter (see page 359), cut 16 shapes from dough; cut in half to make 32 rectangles. Place about 5cm apart on oven trays. Bake 12 minutes.
5 Carefully trim edges of sesame snaps to fit the top of each biscuit. Top each hot biscuit with a sesame snap; bake 3 minutes. Cool on trays.

Makes 32

peanut brittle cookies

125g butter, softened
¼ cup (70g) crunchy
   peanut butter
½ cup (100g) firmly packed
   brown sugar
1 egg
1½ cups (225g) plain flour
½ teaspoon bicarbonate
   of soda
Peanut brittle
¾ cup (100g) roasted
   unsalted peanuts
½ cup (110g) caster sugar
2 tablespoons water

1 Preheat oven to 160°C/140°C fan-forced. Grease oven trays; line with baking paper.
2 Make peanut brittle.
3 Beat butter, peanut butter, sugar and egg in small bowl with electric mixer until combined. Stir in sifted dry ingredients and crushed peanut brittle.
4 Roll heaped teaspoons of mixture into balls with floured hands. Place about 5cm apart on oven trays; flatten slightly with hand.
5 Bake about 12 minutes. Cool on trays.

Peanut brittle
Place nuts on baking-paper-lined oven tray. Combine sugar and the water in small frying pan, stir over heat, without boiling, until sugar is dissolved. Bring to a boil; boil, uncovered, without stirring, until golden brown. Pour mixture over nuts; leave until set. Crush coarsely in food processor.

Makes 42

jaffa jelly cakes

½ cup (110g) caster sugar
2 eggs
1 cup (150g) plain flour
2 tablespoons caster sugar, extra
400g dark eating chocolate,
    melted
3 slices glacé orange,
    cut into wedges
Orange jelly
1 cup (250ml) orange juice
2 tablespoons orange
    marmalade
85g packet orange jelly crystals

1 Make orange jelly.
2 Preheat oven to 180°C/160°C fan-forced. Grease oven trays; line with baking paper.
3 Spread sugar evenly over base of shallow oven tray; heat in oven until sugar feels hot to touch. Beat eggs in small bowl with electric mixer on high speed for 1 minute; add hot sugar, beat about 10 minutes or until mixture is thick and will hold its shape.
4 Meanwhile, sift flour three times. Fit large piping bag with plain 1cm tube.
5 Transfer egg mixture to large bowl, fold in sifted flour. Place mixture into piping bag. Pipe 4cm rounds of mixture onto oven trays, about 3cm apart.
6 Sprinkle each round evenly with extra sugar. Bake each tray, one at a time, about 4 minutes. Cool on trays.
7 Lift jelly from pan to board. Using a 4cm round cutter (see page 359), cut out 25 shapes.
8 Top each sponge with a round of jelly, place on wire rack over tray; coat with chocolate. When chocolate is almost set, top with glacé orange wedges.

Orange jelly
Combine juice and marmalade in small saucepan, bring to a boil; remove from heat. Add jelly crystals, stir until dissolved; cool. Line a deep 23cm-square cake pan with baking paper, extending paper 5cm above edges of pan. Pour jelly into pan; refrigerate until set.

Makes 25

choc ginger easter egg cookies

125g butter, softened
¾ cup (165g) firmly packed
  brown sugar
1 egg
2 tablespoons finely chopped
  glacé ginger
1½ cups (225g) plain flour
¼ cup (35g) self-raising flour
¼ cup (25g) cocoa powder
Chocolate fondant icing
300g chocolate prepared
  fondant, chopped coarsely
1 egg white, beaten lightly
Royal icing
1½ cups (240g) pure icing sugar
1 egg white
pink, green, blue and yellow
  food colouring

1 Beat butter, sugar and egg in small bowl with electric mixer until combined. Stir in ginger then sifted flours and cocoa, in two batches.
2 Knead dough on floured surface until smooth. Roll dough between sheets of baking paper until 5mm thick; refrigerate 30 minutes.
3 Preheat oven to 180°C/160°C fan-forced. Grease oven trays; line with baking paper.
4 Using 2.5cm, 4cm, 5.5cm and 7cm oval cutters (see page 359), cut 13 shapes from dough with each cutter. Place about 3cm apart on oven trays.
5 Bake small cookies about 10 minutes; bake larger cookies about 12 minutes. Cool on wire racks.
6 Make chocolate fondant icing. Use a metal spatula, dipped in hot water, to spread icing quickly over cookies. Set at room temperature.
7 Make royal icing. Divide icing among four bowls. Tint each bowl with food colouring; use to pipe patterns on cookies.

Chocolate fondant icing
Stir fondant in small heatproof bowl over small saucepan of simmering water until smooth. Stir in egg white. Stand at room temperature about 10 minutes or until thickened slightly.

Royal icing
Sift icing sugar through fine sieve. Beat egg white until foamy in small bowl with electric mixer; beat in icing sugar, one tablespoon at a time. Cover surface tightly with plastic wrap.

Makes 52

125g butter, softened
½ cup (110g) caster sugar
1 egg
2 tablespoons golden syrup
2 tablespoons honey
½ cup (45g) rolled oats
½ cup (65g) rolled barley
2 cups (300g) plain flour
½ teaspoon bicarbonate of soda
1½ teaspoons cream of tartar
1 teaspoon ground ginger
1 teaspoon mixed spice
½ teaspoon ground clove
½ cup (45g) rolled oats, extra

1 Preheat oven to 180°C/160°C fan-forced. Grease oven trays; line with baking paper.
2 Beat butter, sugar and egg in small bowl with electric mixer until combined. Transfer to large bowl; stir in golden syrup, honey, oats, barley and sifted dry ingredients.
3 Knead dough on floured surface until smooth. Sprinkle surface with extra rolled oats; roll level tablespoons of dough in oats into 12cm sausages.
4 Shape into horseshoe; place about 3cm apart on oven trays. Bake about 20 minutes. Cool on wire racks.

Makes 26

honey, oat and barley horseshoe cookies

2 x 18g instant latte sachets
1 tablespoon boiling water
125g butter, softened
¾ cup (165g) firmly packed
 brown sugar
1 egg
1½ cups (225g) plain flour
¼ cup (35g) self-raising flour

1 Blend contents of latte sachets with the water in small bowl.
2 Beat butter, sugar, egg and latte paste in small bowl with electric mixer until combined. Stir in sifted flours in two batches.
3 Knead dough on floured surface until smooth; roll dough between sheets of baking paper until 5mm thick. Cover; refrigerate 30 minutes.
4 Preheat oven to 180°C/160°C fan-forced. Grease oven trays; line with baking paper.
5 Using a fancy 7.5cm square cutter (see page 359), cut out 30 squares. Place squares on oven trays. Stamp centre of each cookie with a floured rubber stamp (see page 356).
6 Bake about 15 minutes. Cool on wire racks.

Makes 30

girl-about-town latte cookies

pink macaroons

3 egg whites
2 tablespoons caster sugar
pink food colouring
1¼ cups (200g) icing sugar
1 cup (120g) almond meal
2 tablespoons icing sugar, extra
White chocolate ganache
100g white eating chocolate,
    chopped coarsely
2 tablespoons thickened cream

1 Make white chocolate ganache.
2 Grease oven trays; line with baking paper.
3 Beat egg whites in small bowl with electric mixer until soft peaks form. Add sugar and food colouring, beat until sugar dissolves. Transfer mixture to large bowl. Fold in sifted icing sugar and almond meal, in two batches.
4 Spoon mixture into large piping bag fitted with 1.5cm plain tube. Pipe 36 x 4cm rounds, 2cm apart, onto trays. Tap trays on bench top to allow macaroons to spread slightly. Dust with sifted extra icing sugar; stand 15 minutes.
5 Preheat oven to 150°C/130°C fan-forced.
6 Bake macaroons about 20 minutes. Stand 5 minutes; transfer to wire rack to cool.
7 Sandwich macaroons with ganache. Dust with a little sifted icing sugar, if desired.

White chocolate ganache
Stir chocolate and cream in small saucepan over low heat until smooth. Transfer mixture to small bowl. Cover; refrigerate until mixture is spreadable.

Makes 18

shortbread button cookies

250g butter, softened
⅓ cup (75g) caster sugar
¼ cup (35g) rice flour
2¼ cups (335g) plain flour
1 tablespoon caster sugar, extra

1 Preheat oven to 150°C/130°C fan-forced. Grease oven trays; line with baking paper.
2 Beat butter and sugar in small bowl with electric mixer until smooth. Stir in sifted flours. Knead dough on floured surface until smooth.
3 Place 5cm round floured cutter (see page 359) on an oven tray, press one level tablespoon of dough evenly inside the cutter, remove cutter (see page 356). Repeat with remaining dough.
4 Use the lid of a plastic water bottle to indent the buttons. Use a skewer to make holes in buttons. Use a fork to make pattern around edges of buttons (see page 356).
5 Sprinkle buttons with extra sugar. Bake 30 minutes or until firm. Cool on trays.

Makes 26

caramel ginger crunch cookies

2 cups (300g) plain flour
½ teaspoon bicarbonate of soda
1 teaspoon ground cinnamon
2 teaspoons ground ginger
1 cup (220g) caster sugar
125g cold butter, chopped
1 egg
1 teaspoon golden syrup
2 tablespoons finely chopped
   glacé ginger
45 wrapped hard caramels

1 Preheat oven to 160°C/140°C fan-forced. Grease oven trays; line with baking paper.
2 Process sifted dry ingredients with butter until mixture is crumbly; add egg, golden syrup and ginger, process until ingredients come together. Knead on floured surface until smooth.
3 Roll rounded teaspoons of mixture into balls; flatten slightly. Place about 3cm apart on oven trays.
4 Bake 13 minutes. Place one caramel on top of each hot cookie. Bake about 7 minutes or until caramel begins to melt. Cool on trays.

Makes 45

christmas angel cookies

125g butter, softened
¾ cup (165g) caster sugar
1 egg
1½ cups (225g) plain flour
¼ cup (35g) self-raising flour
½ cup (40g) desiccated coconut
⅓ cup (110g) apricot jam,
  warmed, strained

Macaroon topping
3 egg whites
¾ cup (165g) caster sugar
¼ cup (35g) plain flour
2¼ cups (180g) desiccated
  coconut

1 Beat butter, sugar and egg in small bowl with electric mixer until light and fluffy. Stir in sifted flours and coconut in two batches.
2 Knead dough on floured surface until smooth; roll dough between sheets of baking paper until 5mm thick. Cover; refrigerate 30 minutes.
3 Preheat oven to 180°C/160°C fan-forced. Grease oven trays; line with baking paper.
4 Make macaroon topping.
5 Using 11cm angel cutter (see page 359), cut 16 angel shapes from dough. Place, about 3cm apart, on oven trays.
6 Bake 8 minutes. Spread each hot cookie with jam; divide macaroon topping among angels. Cover with foil (like a tent so foil does not touch surface of macaroon). Bake about 7 minutes. Cool on wire racks.

Macaroon topping
Beat egg whites in small bowl with electric mixer until soft peaks form. Gradually add sugar, beating until dissolved between additions. Fold in sifted flour and coconut in two batches.

Makes 16

green tea and almond tile cookies

125g butter, softened
¼ cup (55g) caster sugar
½ teaspoon vanilla extract
1 egg
1 cup (150g) plain flour
2 tablespoons self-raising flour
¼ cup (35g) cornflour
1 tablespoon green tea leaves
    (about 4 tea bags)
½ cup (60g) almond meal
Fondant icing
300g white prepared fondant,
    chopped coarsely
1 egg white, beaten lightly
Royal icing
1½ cups (240g) pure icing sugar
1 egg white
½ teaspoon vanilla extract
black food colouring

1 Beat butter, sugar, extract
and egg in small bowl with
electric mixer until light and
fluffy. Stir in sifted flours, tea
and almond meal.
2 Knead dough on floured
surface until smooth; roll dough
between sheets of baking
paper until 5mm thick. Cover,
refrigerate 30 minutes.
3 Preheat oven to 180°C/160°C
fan-forced. Grease oven trays;
line with baking paper.
4 Using 9.5cm square cutter
(see page 359), cut 14 squares
from dough. Cut squares in half
to make 28 rectangles. Place
about 3cm apart on oven trays.
5 Bake about 15 minutes. Cool
on wire racks.
6 Make fondant icing. Make
royal icing.
7 Using a metal spatula dipped
in hot water, spread cookies with
fondant icing. Decorate with
black royal icing.

Fondant icing
Stir fondant in small heatproof
bowl over small saucepan of
simmering water until smooth.
Add egg white; stir until smooth.

Royal icing
Sift icing sugar through fine
sieve. Beat egg white until foamy
in small bowl with electric mixer;
add icing sugar, a tablespoon at
a time. When icing reaches firm
peaks, use a wooden spoon to
beat in extract and colouring;
cover surface tightly with
plastic wrap.

Makes 28

frangipani cookies

185g butter, softened
1 teaspoon coconut essence
2 teaspoons finely grated
  lime rind
⅓ cup (75g) caster sugar
1½ cups (225g) plain flour
¼ cup (35g) rice flour
⅓ cup (30g) desiccated coconut
¼ cup (55g) finely chopped
  glacé pineapple
1 tablespoon purple
  coloured sprinkles
Fondant icing
300g white prepared fondant,
  chopped coarsely
1 egg white, beaten lightly
pink food colouring

1 Beat butter, essence, rind and sugar in small bowl with electric mixer until smooth. Stir in sifted flours, coconut and pineapple in two batches.
2 Knead dough on floured surface until smooth. Roll dough between sheets of baking paper until 5mm thick. Refrigerate 30 minutes.
3 Preheat oven to 160°C/140°C fan-forced. Grease round based patty pans.
4 Using 7cm flower cutter (see page 359), cut 28 shapes from dough. Place in patty pans (see page 358).
5 Bake about 10 minutes. Cool in pans.
6 Make fondant icing. Using a metal spatula dipped in hot water, spread pink icing quickly over cookies. Sprinkle coloured sprinkles into centres of flowers.

Fondant icing
Stir fondant in small bowl over small saucepan of simmering water until smooth. Add egg white; stir until smooth. Tint with colouring.

Makes 28

iced marshmallow butterfly cookies

You will need three 250g packets raspberry and vanilla marshmallows for this recipe.

125g butter, softened
¾ cup (165g) caster sugar
1 egg
1½ cups (225g) plain flour
¼ cup (35g) self-raising flour
½ cup (40g) desiccated coconut
⅓ cup (25g) desiccated coconut, extra
Topping
¼ cup (80g) strawberry jam, warmed, strained, cooled
48 pink marshmallows
48 white marshmallows

1 Beat butter, sugar and egg in small bowl with electric mixer until light and fluffy. Stir in sifted flours and coconut, in two batches.
2 Knead dough on floured surface until smooth. Roll dough between sheets of baking paper until 5mm thick; refrigerate 30 minutes.
3 Preheat oven to 180°C/160°C fan-forced. Grease oven trays; line with baking paper.
4 Using 11.5cm butterfly cutter (see page 359), cut 16 shapes from dough. Place about 3cm apart on oven trays. Bake about 12 minutes.
5 Meanwhile, using scissors, quarter marshmallows. Press marshmallows cut-side down onto hot butterfly wings, trim marshmallows to the shape of the wings if necessary. Brush marshmallows with a little water; sprinkle with extra coconut. Bake about 1 minute or until marshmallows soften slightly.
6 Pipe jam down centre of each butterfly. Cool on wire racks.

Makes 16

hazelnut chai teacup cookies

125g butter, softened
1 teaspoon vanilla extract
¼ cup (55g) caster sugar
1 egg yolk
1 cup (150g) plain flour
2 tablespoons self-raising flour
¼ cup (35g) cornflour
1 tablespoon chai tea
   (about 4 chai tea bags)
½ cup (50g) hazelnut meal
Fondant icing
300g white prepared fondant,
   chopped coarsely
1 egg white, beaten lightly
1 teaspoon lemon juice
yellow, blue and green
   food colouring
Royal icing
1½ cups (240g) pure icing sugar
1 egg white

1 Preheat oven to 180°C/160°C fan-forced. Grease oven trays; line with baking paper.
2 Beat butter, extract, sugar and egg yolk in small bowl with electric mixer until light and fluffy. Stir in sifted flours, tea and hazelnut meal.
3 Knead dough on floured surface until smooth; roll dough between sheets of baking paper until 5mm thick.
4 Using 8.5cm teacup cutter, cut out 14 shapes from dough. Place about 3cm apart on oven trays. Bake about 15 minutes. Cool on trays.
5 Make fondant icing. Using a metal spatula dipped in hot water, spread icing quickly over cookies.
6 Make royal icing. Decorate cookies with royal icing.

Fondant icing
Stir fondant in small heatproof bowl over small saucepan of simmering water until smooth; stir in egg white and juice. Divide among three bowls; tint yellow, blue and green with food colouring.

Royal icing
Sift icing sugar through fine sieve. Beat egg white until foamy in small bowl with electric mixer; beat in icing sugar a tablespoon at a time. Cover surface tightly with plastic wrap.

Makes 14

hazelnut shortbread trees

250g butter, softened
2 teaspoons finely grated
   orange rind
½ cup (80g) icing sugar
2 tablespoons rice flour
2 cups (300g) plain flour
2 teaspoons mixed spice
¼ cup (75ml) hazelnut meal
silver cachous
1 tablespoon icing sugar, extra
Brandy butter cream
60g butter, softened
½ teaspoon finely grated
   orange rind
¾ cup (120g) icing sugar
2 teaspoons brandy

1 Beat butter, rind and sifted icing sugar in small bowl with electric mixer until light and fluffy. Transfer to large bowl. Stir in sifted flours and spice, and hazelnut meal, in two batches.
2 Knead dough on floured surface until smooth. Roll dough between sheets of baking paper until 5mm thick; refrigerate 30 minutes.
3 Preheat oven to 180°C/160°C fan-forced. Grease oven trays; line with baking paper.
4 Using 3cm, 5cm and 7cm star-shaped cutters (see page 359), cut 24 of each size star from dough. Place small stars, about 1cm apart, on an oven tray; place remaining stars, about 2cm apart, on oven trays.
5 Bake small stars about 10 minutes. Bake larger stars about 15 minutes. Stand 5 minutes; cool on wire racks.
6 Meanwhile, make brandy butter cream.

7 Sandwich two of each size cookie with butter cream. Assemble trees by joining three different size stars together with butter cream.
8 Decorate trees by joining cachous to stars with a tiny dot of butter cream. Dust trees with extra sifted icing sugar.

Brandy butter cream
Beat butter, rind, sifted icing sugar and brandy in small bowl with electric mixer until light and fluffy.

Makes 12

checkerboard cookies

200g butter, softened
¾ cup (165g) caster sugar
½ teaspoon vanilla extract
1 egg
2 cups (300g) plain flour
1 tablespoon cocoa powder
1 teaspoon finely grated
orange rind
¼ cup (40g) finely chopped
dried cranberries
1 egg white, beaten lightly

1 Beat butter, sugar, extract and egg in small bowl with electric mixer until light and fluffy. Stir in sifted flour in two batches.
2 Divide dough in half, knead sifted cocoa into one half; knead rind and cranberries into the other half. Using ruler, shape each batch of dough into 4.5cm x 4.5cm x 15cm rectangular bars (see page 357). Wrap each in baking paper; refrigerate 30 minutes.
3 Cut each bar lengthways equally into three slices. Cut each slice lengthways equally into three; you will have nine 1.5cm x 1.5cm x 1.5cm slices of each dough (see page 357).

4 Brush each slice of dough with egg white, stack alternate flavours together in threes. Stick three stacks together to recreate the log; repeat with second log (see page 357). Refrigerate 30 minutes.
5 Preheat oven to 180°C/160°C fan-forced. Grease oven trays; line with baking paper.
6 Using a sharp knife, cut each log into 1cm slices (see page 357). Place, cut-side up, on oven trays about 3cm apart. Bake about 15 minutes. Stand 5 minutes before lifting onto wire racks to cool.

Makes 30

baby shape cookies

125g butter, softened
2 teaspoons finely grated
    orange rind
¼ cup (55g) caster sugar
1 egg yolk
1 cup (150g) plain flour
2 tablespoons self-raising flour
¼ cup (35g) cornflour
½ cup (60g) almond meal
1 tablespoon finely chopped
    dried lavender or dried
    rose buds
Lemon icing
1 egg white
1½ cups (240g) icing sugar
2 teaspoons plain flour
2 teaspoons lemon juice,
    approximately
blue food colouring
Royal icing
1½ cups (240g) pure icing sugar
1 egg white
blue food colouring

1 Beat butter, rind, sugar and egg yolk in small bowl with electric mixer until light and fluffy. Stir in sifted flours, almond meal and lavender or rose.
2 Knead dough on floured surface until smooth; roll between sheets of baking paper until 5mm thick. Cover; refrigerate 30 minutes.
3 Preheat oven to 180°C/160°C fan-forced. Grease oven trays; line with baking paper.
4 Using 12.5cm bottle and 11cm pram cutters (see page 359), cut 7 shapes of each from dough. Place about 3cm apart on oven trays.
5 Bake about 12 minutes. Cool on trays.
6 Make lemon icing; spread icing evenly over cookies.
7 Make royal icing. Decorate cookies with royal icing.

Lemon icing
Place egg white in small bowl, stir in half the sifted icing sugar; stir in remaining sifted icing sugar, flour and enough juice to make a thick, spreadable icing. Divide icing among two bowls; tint one bowl with blue food colouring.

Royal icing
Sift icing sugar through fine sieve. Beat egg white until foamy in small bowl with electric mixer; beat in icing sugar a tablespoon at a time. Divide icing among two bowls; tint one bowl with blue food colouring. Cover surface of icing tightly with plastic wrap.

Makes 14

choc-mallow wheels

You will need a 250g packet of raspberry and vanilla marshmallows for this recipe.

125g butter, softened
¾ cup (165g) firmly packed brown sugar
1 egg
1½ cups (225g) plain flour
¼ cup (35g) self-raising flour
¼ cup (25g) cocoa powder
28 marshmallows
¼ cup (80g) raspberry jam
375g dark chocolate Melts
1 tablespoon vegetable oil

1 Beat butter, sugar and egg in small bowl with electric mixer until combined. Stir in sifted flours and cocoa, in two batches.
2 Knead dough on floured surface until smooth. Roll between sheets of baking paper until 3mm thick. Cover; refrigerate 30 minutes.
3 Preheat oven to 180°C/160°C fan-forced. Grease oven trays; line with baking paper.
4 Using 7cm round fluted cutter, cut 28 rounds from dough. Place about 3cm apart on trays.
5 Bake about 12 minutes. Cool on wire racks.
6 Turn half the biscuits base-side up; place on oven tray. Use scissors to cut marshmallows in half horizontally. Press four marshmallow halves, cut-side down, onto biscuit bases on tray. Bake 2 minutes.

7 Melt chocolate in medium heatproof bowl over medium saucepan of simmering water. Remove from heat; stir in oil.
8 Spread jam over bases of remaining cookies; press onto softened marshmallow. Stand 20 minutes or until marshmallow is firm. Dip wheels into chocolate; smooth away excess chocolate using metal spatula. Place on baking-paper-lined trays to set.

Makes 14

passionfruit cookies

1 cup (150g) plain flour
½ cup (75g) self-raising flour
2 tablespoons custard powder
⅔ cup (110g) icing sugar
90g cold butter, chopped
1 egg yolk
¼ cup (60ml) passionfruit pulp
Butter icing
125g unsalted butter, softened
1½ cups (240g) icing sugar
2 tablespoons milk

1 Process dry ingredients and butter together until crumbly; add egg yolk and passionfruit pulp, pulse until ingredients come together.
2 Knead dough on floured surface until smooth. Roll between sheets of baking paper until 5mm thick; refrigerate 30 minutes.
3 Preheat oven to 180°C/160°C fan-forced. Grease oven trays; line with baking paper.
4 Using 4cm round flower-shaped cutter (see page 359), cut rounds from dough. Place about 3cm apart on oven trays.
5 Bake about 10 minutes. Cool on wire racks.
6 Make butter icing.
7 Spoon icing into piping bag fitted with a small fluted tube. Pipe stars onto cookies.

Butter icing
Beat butter in small bowl with electric mixer until as white as possible. Gradually beat in half the sifted icing sugar, milk, then remaining icing sugar.

Makes 70

250g butter, softened
1¼ cups (200g) icing sugar
1 teaspoon vanilla extract
2 cups (300g) plain flour
½ cup (75g) rice flour
⅓ cup (50g) cornflour
2 tablespoons milk

1 Beat butter, sifted icing sugar and extract in small bowl with electric mixer until light and fluffy. Transfer to large bowl; stir in sifted flours, in two batches, then milk.
2 Divide mixture in half. Knead each half on floured surface until smooth, then roll each half into 25cm logs. Wrap each log in baking paper; refrigerate about 1 hour or until firm.
3 Preheat oven to 160°C/140°C fan-forced. Grease oven trays; line with baking paper.
4 Cut the logs into 1cm slices; place about 3cm apart on oven trays. Bake about 20 minutes. Cool on wire racks.

Makes 48

Variations
Orange and poppy seed
Omit vanilla extract; beat 1 tablespoon finely grated orange rind with butter and sugar. Add 2 tablespoons poppy seeds with sifted flours.

Lemon and cranberry
Omit vanilla extract; beat 1 tablespoon finely grated lemon rind with butter and sugar. Stir in ¾ cup (100g) coarsely chopped dried cranberries with sifted flours.

Pecan and cinnamon
Add 1 teaspoon ground cinnamon to sifted flours, then stir in 1 cup (120g) coarsely chopped pecans. Sprinkle with cinnamon sugar before baking.

M&M's
Stir in 2 x 35g packets of mini M&M's with sifted flours.

slice and bake cookies

coffee walnut cream cookies

1⅔ cups (250g) plain flour
125g cold butter, chopped
¼ cup (55g) caster sugar
½ teaspoon vanilla extract
1 egg, beaten lightly
18 walnut halves
Walnut butter cream
185g unsalted butter, softened
¾ cup (120g) icing sugar
1 tablespoon cocoa
1 tablespoon instant
    coffee granules
1 tablespoon hot water
1¼ cups (125g) walnuts,
    chopped finely
Coffee icing
1 cup (160g) icing sugar
2 teaspoons instant
    coffee granules
1 tablespoon hot water
1 teaspoon butter

1 Sift flour into medium bowl, rub in butter. Stir in sugar, extract and egg.
2 Knead dough on floured surface until smooth. Divide in half. Roll, in half between sheets of baking paper until 3mm thick. Refrigerate 30 minutes.
3 Preheat oven to 180°C/160°C fan-forced. Grease oven trays; line with baking paper.
4 Using 5.5cm round cutter (see page 359), cut out 36 rounds. Place on oven trays; bake about 12 minutes. Cool on wire racks.
5 Meanwhile, make walnut butter cream.
6 Sandwich cookies with butter cream; refrigerate 30 minutes.
7 Meanwhile, make coffee icing.
8 Spread cookies with icing and top with walnut halves.

Walnut butter cream
Beat butter and sifted icing sugar in small bowl with electric mixer until light and fluffy. Beat in combined cocoa, coffee and the water. Stir in nuts.

Coffee icing
Sift icing sugar into small heatproof bowl, stir in combined coffee and the water; add butter. Stir over small saucepan of simmering water until icing is spreadable.

Makes 18

3 egg whites
¾ cup (165g) caster sugar
1¼ cups (120g) hazelnut meal
1½ cups (185g) almond meal
¼ cup (35g) plain flour
100g dark eating chocolate,
    melted

1 Preheat oven to 160°C/140°C fan-forced. Grease oven trays; line with baking paper.
2 Beat egg whites in small bowl with electric mixer until foamy. Gradually beat in sugar, one tablespoon at a time, until dissolved between additions. Transfer mixture to large bowl.
3 Fold in nut meals and sifted flour. Spoon mixture into large piping bag fitted with 1.5cm plain tube. Pipe 8cm sticks onto trays.
4 Bake about 15 minutes. Cool on trays 5 minutes; place on wire racks to cool.
5 Drizzle sticks with melted chocolate, place on baking-paper-lined trays to set.

Makes 34

nutty meringue sticks

pistachio shortbread mounds

⅔ cup (70g) shelled
  pistachios, roasted
250g butter, softened
1 cup (160g) icing sugar
1½ cups (225g) plain flour
2 tablespoons rice flour
2 tablespoons cornflour
¾ cup (90g) almond meal
⅓ cup (55g) icing sugar, extra

1 Preheat oven to 150°C/130°C fan-forced. Grease oven trays; line with baking paper.
2 Coarsely chop half the nuts.
3 Beat butter and sifted icing sugar in small bowl with electric mixer until light and fluffy; transfer to large bowl. Stir in sifted flours, almond meal and chopped nuts.
4 Shape level tablespoons of mixture into mounds; place about 3cm apart on oven trays. Press one whole nut on each mound; bake about 25 minutes. Stand 5 minutes; place on wire racks to cool. Serve dusted with extra sifted icing sugar.

Makes 35

chocolate lady's kisses

80g butter, softened
½ teaspoon vanilla extract
¼ cup (55g) caster sugar
1 egg
½ cup (50g) hazelnut meal
¾ cup (110g) plain flour
¼ cup (25g) cocoa powder
1 tablespoon cocoa powder, extra
Choc-hazelnut cream
100g dark eating chocolate,
  melted
50g butter
⅓ cup (110g) chocolate
  hazelnut spread

1 Beat butter, extract, sugar and egg in small bowl with electric mixer until combined. Stir in hazelnut meal, then sifted flour and cocoa.
2 Roll dough between sheets of baking paper until 3mm thick. Refrigerate 1 hour.
3 Make choc-hazelnut cream.
4 Preheat oven to 180°C/160°C fan-forced. Grease oven trays; line with baking paper.
5 Using 4cm fluted cutter, cut 52 rounds from dough. Place on oven trays.
6 Bake about 8 minutes. Stand 5 minutes; place on wire racks to cool.
7 Spoon choc-hazelnut cream into piping bag fitted with large fluted tube. Pipe cream onto one biscuit; top with another biscuit. Repeat with remaining biscuits and cream. Dust with extra sifted cocoa.

Choc-hazelnut cream
Beat cooled chocolate, butter and spread in small bowl with electric mixer until thick and glossy.

Makes 26

250g butter, softened
1 teaspoon vanilla extract
½ cup (110g) firmly packed
   brown sugar
1 cup (220g) caster sugar
2 eggs
2¾ cups (410g) plain flour
1 teaspoon bicarbonate of soda
½ teaspoon ground nutmeg
1 tablespoon caster sugar, extra
2 teaspoons ground cinnamon

1 Beat butter, extract and sugars in small bowl with electric mixer until light and fluffy. Add eggs, one at a time, beating until combined. Transfer to large bowl.
2 Stir in sifted flour, soda and nutmeg, in two batches. Cover; refrigerate 30 minutes.
3 Preheat oven to 180°C/160°C fan-forced. Grease oven trays; line with baking paper.
4 Combine extra caster sugar and cinnamon in small shallow bowl. Roll level tablespoons of the dough into balls; roll balls in cinnamon sugar. Place balls about 7cm apart on oven trays.
5 Bake about 12 minutes. Cool on trays.

Makes 42

snickerdoodles

praline custard cream cookies

1 cup (150g) plain flour
1¼ cups (90g) almond meal
90g cold butter, chopped
1 egg yolk
1 teaspoon vanilla extract
2 tablespoons icing sugar
Custard filling
⅓ cup (75g) caster sugar
¼ cup (35g) plain flour
2 egg yolks
1 cup (250ml) milk
125g butter, softened
1 teaspoon vanilla extract
½ cup (80g) icing sugar
Almond praline
½ cup (40g) flaked almonds
½ cup (110g) caster sugar
2 tablespoons water

1 Make custard filling and almond praline.
2 Preheat oven to 160°C/140°C fan-forced. Grease oven trays; line with baking paper.
3 Process flour, meal and butter until crumbly. Add egg yolk and extract; pulse until combined.
4 Knead dough on floured surface until smooth. Roll dough between sheets of baking paper until 3mm thick.
5 Using 3.5cm round cutter (see page 359), cut 72 rounds from dough. Place about 2cm apart on oven trays. Bake about 12 minutes. Cool on trays.
6 Sandwich cookies with custard filling. Spread a little more custard filling around side of cookies. Roll cookies in praline then dust with sifted icing sugar.

Custard filling
Combine sugar and flour in small saucepan; gradually stir in combined yolks and milk until smooth. Cook, stirring, until mixture boils and thickens. Simmer, stirring, over low heat, 1 minute; remove from heat. Cover surface of custard with plastic wrap; refrigerate until cold. Beat butter and extract until mixture is as white as possible. Beat in sifted icing sugar. Beat in cooled custard, in four batches, until smooth.

Almond praline
Place nuts on baking-paper-lined oven tray. Combine sugar and the water in small fying pan; stir over heat, without boiling, until sugar is dissolved. Bring to a boil; boil, uncovered, without stirring, until golden brown. Pour toffee over nuts; set at room temperature. Crush praline finely in food processor.

Makes 36

cupcake tips

Melting chocolate

Place coarsely chopped chocolate in small heatproof bowl, over small saucepan of simmering water; stir occasionally, until chocolate is melted. It is important that water not be allowed to come in contact with the chocolate, if it does it will sieze. You can melt chocolate in a microwave oven; melt on MEDIUM (55%) about 1 minute, stirring twice during melting.

Making small chocolate curls

Using a sharp vegetable peeler, scrape along the side of a long piece of room-temperature eating-quality chocolate. Clean the peeler often so that the chocolate doesn't clog the surface of the blade.

Making chocolate curls using melon baller

Spread melted chocolate evenly and thinly onto a piece of marble, laminated board or flat oven tray; stand at room temperature until just set but not hard. Pull a melon baller over the surface of chocolate to make curls. We used these as gum nuts (see page 105).

Painting foil cases & leaves with chocolate

Use a fine clean, dry paintbrush. Paint melted chocolate thickly inside each foil case or onto one side of a clean freshly-picked leaf; leave to set at room temperature.

Finishing chocolate foil cases & leaves

Carefully peel back case or leaf from chocolate. These can be made ahead and stored in an airtight container at room temperature until required. If the weather is hot, keep them in the refrigerator.

Colouring white chocolate

Using a skewer, add a few drops of colouring (the amount depends on the intensity of the colouring) into melted white chocolate and stir with a clean dry spoon, until colour is even. Too much colouring will cause chocolate to seize, that is, clump and turn an unappealing colour.

Making a piping bag

Cut a 30cm square of baking or greaseproof paper in half diagonally; hold apex of one triangle towards you. Twist first one point, then the other, into a cone shape. Bring three points together; secure the three points with a staple; repeat with other triangle. Sticky tape will hold a greaseproof bag together, but not one made from baking paper.

Piping chocolate

Place melted chocolate into paper piping bag. Snip end from bag. Cover an oven tray with baking paper, pipe desired shapes; leave to set at room temperature. Gently lift chocolate shapes from paper.

Making sugar syrup

Always place sugar and water in recommended size heavy-based saucepan. To prevent crystallisation or graininess, the sugar must be completely dissolved before the mixture boils. Stir constantly over medium to high heat to dissolve sugar. If sugar grains stick to the side of the pan, use a clean pastry brush dipped in water to brush down the sides of the pan.

Boiling sugar syrup

After sugar syrup comes to a boil, do not stir, and do not scrape pan or stir the syrup during cooking. Boil the syrup for about 5 minutes or until thick. Remove pan from heat; allow bubbles to subside before using. This stage can be measured accurately by buying a candy thermometer. The temperature should be 118°C. This stage is perfect for fluffy frosting.

Boiling sugar syrup to hard crack

Bring sugar syrup to a boil, reduce heat; simmer uncovered, without stirring for about 10 minutes or until mixture is golden. Remove from heat; stand until bubbles subside before using. If using a candy thermometer, mixture should be between 138°C and 154°C depending on the colour required. The longer the toffee boils and colours the harder it will set.

Candy thermometer

Thermometer should be stainless steel and have a clip to attach to the pan. Once sugar is dissolved, place thermometer in small saucepan of cold water (mercury must be covered). Bring the water to a boil, check thermometer for accuracy at boiling point. When sugar syrup comes to a boil, place thermometer in syrup (mercury must be covered). Boil to the required temperature. Return thermometer to pan of boiling water, remove from heat, allow thermometer to cool in the water.

Checking toffee for hard crack

To test toffee for hard crack use a clean dry spoon and carefully drizzle some toffee into cold water. If it has reached hard crack it should set immediately. Always remove the pan from the heat and allow the bubbles to subside before testing.

Testing toffee

Remove set toffee from cold water and snap between fingers. It should be brittle and snap easily.

Making toffee shards

When toffee reaches a golden colour, remove pan from heat, allow bubbles to subside; drizzle toffee from the back of a wooden spoon, onto a baking-paper-lined oven tray. Allow toffee to set at room temperature. Remove shards from paper using a spatula. Immediately position on cake.

Shaping toffee over rolling pin

When toffee reaches a golden colour, remove pan from heat, allow bubbles to subside. Drizzle toffee from wooden spoon onto a rolling pin, covered with baking paper. Allow toffee to set at room temperature. Slide baking paper off rolling pin to remove toffee shapes. Immediately position on cake.

Colouring prepared fondant

After kneading fondant until smooth, use a skewer to colour fondant; kneading colouring into fondant until desired colour is achieved. The amount of colouring needed will depend on the intensity of the colouring used.

Covering cakes with prepared almond paste or fondant

Brush cakes lightly and evenly with jam. Roll almond paste or fondant to desired thickness; lift onto cake with hands or rolling pin. Smooth surface with hands dusted with icing sugar, ease paste or fondant around side and base of cake; trim excess with sharp knife.

Shaping flowers from modelling fondant

Cut out flowers using cutter of choice, place flower on clean folded tea towel. Using ball tool, gently shape flower; leave to dry.

Making butterfy from modelling fondant

Roll out fondant to 2mm thick. Cut out wings, place damp wire into each wing; dry flat. Make body of butterfly by moulding a piece of fondant; attach wire to body.

Shaping butterfly

Bring wires, with wings attached, together. Use florist tape to secure wires and shape butterfly.

Making lily petals from modelling fondant

Knead fondant; roll to a thickness of 2mm. Using the lily petal cutter, cut out 6 petals for each flower. Frill along each edge, using thicker edge of frilling tool. Gently score two lines on each petal.

Drying lily petals

Dry individual petals in round-based patty pans or soup spoons. Bend the wire at a 90° angle from the petal.

Assembling lily

Wet one end of single wire lengths, insert into end of each petal; dry on baking-paper-lined tray. For flower centre (pistle), roll tiny balls of fondant. Wet one end of single wire length, insert into balls; pinch balls several times with tweezers. To assemble lily, attach five stamens to pistle with florist tape. Attach one to two petals at a time, around pistle, using florist tape.

Piping choux pastry
Spoon choux pastry into piping bag fitted with a 1cm plain tube. Hold piping bag vertical to baking-paper-lined oven tray; quickly pivot wrist, piping tiny dollops (equal to ¼ teaspoon) of choux pastry 2cm apart, onto tray.

Piping meringue
Spoon meringue into piping bag fitted with a 1cm plain tube. Hold piping bag vertical to the cake, piping a spiral from the outside to the centre of the cake.

Piping lines with royal icing
Spoon icing into piping bag fitted with a small plain tube. Gently touch surface with tip of tube, lightly squeezing piping bag. As icing comes out, lift tube up from surface, squeezing to desired length. Stop squeezing bag, placing icing down onto surface. Even pressure is paramount – too much will give uneven thickness, too little pressure and the line will break.

Piping cornelli pattern with royal icing
Spoon icing into piping bag fitted with a small plain tube. Hold tube tip close to cake surface so that icing attaches without tube scraping cake or flattening the icing line. Pipe a continuous, meandering line of icing; move tip up, around and down to produce a lacy effect – don't let lines touch or cross.

Piping basket weave with royal icing

Using a basket weave tube, pipe a long vertical line from the top of the cake to the bottom, followed by short horizontal lines across the long vertical line. The horizontal lines should be a tube-width apart.

Pipe the next long vertical line at the end of the previous short horizontal lines.

Pipe short horizontal lines into the gaps, between the two vertical lines.

Repeat previous steps, continuing the basket weave design until the design meets with the starting point.

Shaping cakes
Using a serrated knife carefully shave edges of cake away.

Sugar-frosting fruit
Using a small clean paint brush, lightly and sparingly brush fruit individually with egg white; dip wet fruit in sugar. Place frosted fruit on baking paper-lined tray. Leave about 1 hour or until sugar is dry.

Dusting-on designs
The best results are achieved by using several doilies still joined together, pieces of plastic backed lace tablecloths or thick fabric lace, as they are easier to lift away from the cake once dusted with icing sugar.

Feather and fan
Place chocolate topping into paper piping bag. Starting in the centre of the cream topped cake, pipe a spiral. Using a skewer, gently drag through the spiral design, from the cake centre to the edge of the paper case.

Drying pears and pineapple

Fruit needs to be sliced thinly and evenly – a mandoline or V-slicer is ideal, alternatively use a very sharp knife. Using a clean pastry brush, brush both sides of sliced fruit with sugar syrup. Place fruit on wire rack over an oven tray. Bake for specified time.

Shaping dried pears and pineapple

Dried fruit slices must be lifted from wire rack immediately after baking to prevent sticking. For pear slices, shape by pinching narrow end; dry on wire rack. For pineapple slices, pinch centre of each slice; dry over egg carton.

Colouring sugar

Use granulated or caster sugar, depending on the texture you prefer. Place required amount of sugar in a plastic bag, add a tiny amount of colouring; work colouring through sugar by 'massaging' plastic bag. Sugar will keep in a jar at room temperature indefinitely.

Marking fondant

Roll fondant to desired thickness; place textured templates onto fondant, pressing gently to leave an imprint. Lift template away from fondant. Or, gently press cardboard stencil into fondant, leaving imprint. Paint imprint with colouring or fill with coloured sugar or sprinkles. Or, using a small, clean brush, paint design on stamp with coloured paste; gently press stamp onto fondant, to leave a coloured imprint.

cheesecake tips

Cheesecakes are easy to make, and, with the help of these tips, you will have perfect results every time. Baked cheesecakes should be cooled slowly – turn the oven off after they're cooked, then prop the oven door slightly open, using a wooden spoon. Most cheesecakes benefit from being made a day ahead, the flavours develop and the texture becomes firm. Baked cheesecakes are best eaten at room temperature. Use a hot dry sharp knife to cut cheesecakes.

Using a springform tin for cheesecakes eliminates the turning-out process. If you're going to transfer a cheesecake from a springform tin base to a plate, it's a good idea to secure the base upside down in the tin. This will make it easy to push a large spatula or egg slide under the crust, so you can slide the chilled cheesecake onto a plate.

Lining a springform tin with plastic wrap will give chilled cheesecakes a smooth side. Remove the base of the tin. Drape a long strip of plastic wrap over the lightly greased tin, then position and secure the base back into the tin. This will stretch the wrap neatly, leave a little of the wrap hanging over the edge.

Making a crumb crust that looks good and cuts well depends on fine biscuit crumbs being pressed firmly and evenly into the tin. We use a processor to make fine crumbs, add the butter etc, then pulse to combine ingredients. Press crumbs over the base, then, using a straight-sided glass, press crumbs up the side of the tin.

Beating a cheesecake mixture for a smooth textured result: have the cream cheese, and preferably the other ingredients, at room temperature, before you start to mix. Use the correct sized equipment, and add the ingredients in the order we suggest. Do not over-beat mixtures that contain cream and mascarpone in particular.

Roasting or toasting nuts and coconut is easily done in a frying pan or on an oven tray. Spread the nuts in pan or tray, stir over a medium heat (or, roast in a moderate oven for about 5 minutes) until they're almost as browned as you want them. Spread them out onto a tray to cool.

cookie tips

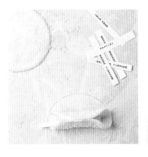  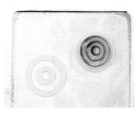 

Coconut fortune cookies, page 249
Make sure you have all your messages ready. As soon as the cookies are baked, remove them from the oven; quickly slide a knife or spatula blade under each cookie to loosen them, then enclose a message in each.

Quickly position each warm cookie over the rim of a glass for 30 seconds to shape; place on wire racks to cool completely.

Stained-glass lollypop cookies, page 262
Using 1.5cm round cutter, cut out 12 rounds from dough, place about 5cm apart on baking-paper-lined oven trays. Starting from the centres of the cookies, use graduating sized round cutters to cut out lollypop shapes (see recipe). Remove excess dough from lollypops.

Brush dough evenly but lightly with lightly beaten egg white, then sprinkle with hundreds and thousands if you like. Slide a paddle pop stick under the circles of dough to the centre of each lollypop. Proceed with recipe.

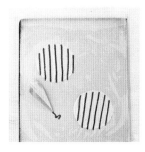   

Ice-cream cone cookies, page 266

Spread one level tablespoon of the plain mixture into the marked circles on the baking-paper-lined oven trays. Fill a paper piping bag (see page 358) with chocolate mixture, snip end of bag, pipe chocolate stripes across the circles.

As soon as shapes feel slightly firm (not crisp) in the oven, remove the tray from the oven. Working quickly, slide a knife or spatula blade und pe. Place on a wire rack to cool completely.

Jigsaw gingerbread people, page 281

Cut out paper shapes from template (available from craft shops). Place half the rolled out dough, still on its baking paper, onto an oven tray, position paper cut-outs from the template on the dough. Using sharp pointed vegetable knife, carefully cut around the shapes.

Carefully pull excess dough away from jigsaw shapes. Gently knead scraps of dough together on lightly floured surface. Re-roll dough between sheets of baking paper to make more jigsaw shapes.

   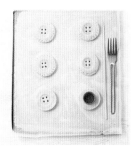

Mud cake cookie sandwiches, page 282

Make a heart-shaped template from light cardboard, large enough to completely cover the top of the sandwiches. Place cocoa into a fine sieve, shake into the heart shape. Carefully remove template. Repeat with the remaining sandwiches.

Girl-about-town latte cookies, page 301

To mark the squares clearly, use well-defined stamps such as high-heeled shoes, lips, handbags etc. Dip the stamps in flour, shake away any excess, then use to mark the squares of dough. Be sure to keep the stamps clean and re-flour between each use.

Shortbread button cookies, page 305

To make neat buttons, place 5cm round floured cutter on baking-paper-lined oven tray. Using a small teaspoon, press one level tablespoon of dough evenly inside the cutter. Remove cutter, wipe, dip in flour again, repeat with remaining dough.

To mark indented centres of buttons, use the lid of a plastic water bottle, dipped in flour. Mark holes in buttons using a bamboo skewer or knitting needle. Use a floured fork to gently mark pattern around edges of buttons.

Checkerboard cookies, page 321

Using the side of a plastic ruler, push and shape each piece of dough into the same size rectangular bar shape. Make sure all the sides of both bars are the same height, depth and width. Wrap each bar in baking paper; refrigerate 30 minutes.

Cut each bar lengthways into three even slices, cut each slice into three lengths. You should have nine lengths from each bar.

Stack alternate flavours of lengths of dough, brushing each length of dough lightly but evenly with egg white as you stack. Start with three lengths, building up to nine lengths in each stack. Wrap each bar in baking paper; refrigerate 30 minutes.

Use a sharp knife to cut bars into 1cm-thick slices; place cut-side-up, about 2cm apart, onto baking-paper-lined oven trays.

Frangipani cookies, page 313
Using 7cm flower cutter (see page 359), cut out flower shapes from rolled-out dough. Place flowers into lightly greased round-based patty pans. Bake as directed in recipe. Cool flowers in pan.

The "Push" test
Most cookies baked on an oven tray should feel a little soft after they've been removed from the oven, they become firm when they cool. If you're in doubt about the firmness, remove the cookies from the oven, then "push" one of the cookies on the tray: if it slides, it's done, if it sticks, it needs more baking.

Paper piping bag
Cut a triangle (with all sides the same length) from greaseproof or baking paper. With the apex of the triangle pointing towards you, twist the triangle into a cone shape, by bringing all three points of the triangle together.

Fold the points over, secure with a staple or sticky tape. Two-thirds fill the bag with icing etc, then fold the top of the bag over to enclose the filling. Snip a tiny piece from the end of the bag ready for piping.

We have used a wide variety of metal cutters, all shapes and sizes, throughout this book. They are available from cake decorator's shops, cookware shops, some department stores and craft shops.
The measurements of the cutters used in the recipes were taken by measuring the longest/widest part of the cutter, for example, we measured a square cutter diagonally.

glossary

after dinner mints mint squares coated in dark chocolate.

almonds
blanched brown skins removed.
essence synthetically produced; made with almond oil and alcohol.
flaked paper-thin slices.
meal also called ground almonds.
slivered small lengthways-cut pieces.

apple juice concentrate made by extracting the juice from the fruit, then pasteurised and evaporated under vacuum. Available at health food stores.

baileys irish cream an irish whiskey and cream-based liqueur.

baking powder a raising agent consisting mainly of two parts cream of tartar to one part bicarbonate of soda (baking soda).

bicarbonate of soda or baking soda.

biscuits
brandy snap is a crisp wafer thin sweet biscuit.
butternut snap crunchy biscuit made from rolled oats, coconut and golden syrup.
chocolate chip plain butter biscuits with chocolate chips.
chocolate cream-filled chocolate biscuits sandwiched together with vanilla cream.
granita also known as digestives; made from wheat flakes.

plain chocolate crunchy biscuit made from cocoa.
plain sweet un-iced sweet vanilla-flavoured biscuits or cookies used to make crumbs.

butter use salted or unsalted ('sweet') butter; 125g equals 1 stick of butter.

cachous small, round cake-decorating sweets available in various colours.

cardamom native to India; can be purchased in pod, seed or ground form. Has a distinctive aromatic, sweetly rich flavour.

chai tea tea drink of India made with a melange of spices ranging from pepper to cardamom to cinnamon.

cheese
cream also called philadelphia or philly; a soft cow-milk cheese with a 14 to 33 per cent fat content.
cottage fresh, white, unripened curd cheese with a lumpy consistency and mild, sweet flavour. Fat content ranges from 15 to 55 per cent, depending whether it is made from whole, low-fat or fat-free cow milk.
low-fat cottage fat content 1 per cent.
low-fat ricotta fat content 9 per cent.
mascarpone an Italian fresh cultured-cream product made in much the same way as yogurt. It is whiteish to creamy yellow in colour, with a buttery-rich, luscious texture.

ricotta a soft, sweet, moist, white cow-milk cheese with a low-fat content (about 11 per cent) and a slightly grainy texture. Its name roughly translates as "cooked again" as its made from a whey that is itself a by-product of other cheese making.

chilli, red thai also called "scuds"; fresh, tiny, very hot and bright red.

chocolate
cherry ripe dark chocolate bar made with coconut and cherries; standard size bar weighs 55g.
dark Bits also called chocolate chips; hold their shape in baking and are ideal for decorating.
dark eating made of cocoa liquor, cocoa butter and sugar.
liqueur we used Cadbury cream liqueur, a chocolate-flavoured liqueur.
Melts discs made of milk, white or dark compound chocolate; good for melting and moulding.
milk eating most popular eating chocolate, mild and very sweet; similar in make-up to dark, differing only by the addition of milk solids.
white eating contains no cocoa solids, deriving its sweet flavour from cocoa butter. Is very sensitive to heat.

chocolate hazelnut spread also known as Nutella.

cinnamon stick dried inner bark of the shoots of a cinnamon tree.

cloves dried flower buds of a tropical tree; can be used whole or in ground form. Has a strong scent and taste so should be used minimally.

cocoa powder also known as cocoa.

coconut

desiccated unsweetened and concentrated, dried finely shredded.

essence synthetically produced from flavouring, oil and alcohol.

flaked dried flaked coconut flesh.

milk not the liquid found inside the fruit (coconut water), but the diluted liquid from the second pressing of the white flesh of a mature coconut. Available in cans and cartons at most supermarkets.

shredded strips of dried coconut flesh.

coffee-flavoured liqueur we used either Tia Maria or Kahlua.

cointreau orange-flavoured liqueur.

coloured sprinkles also called Dollar 5's.

corella pears also called forelle; small to medium in size with a reddish-yellow skin.

cornflour also called cornstarch.

cranberries

dried packaged like raisins and sultanas; available in supermarkets.

fresh tart, red, edible berries.

cream of tartar the acid ingredient in baking powder; added to confectionery mixtures to help prevent sugar crystallising. Keeps frostings creamy and improves volume when beating egg whites.

crème de menthe a sweet, mint-flavoured liqueur.

custard powder instant mixture used to make pouring custard; similar to North American instant pudding mix.

dark rum we use an underproof rum (not overproof) for its subtle flavour.

dried currants dried tiny, almost black raisins so-named from the grape type native to Corinth, Greece. These are not the same as fresh currants, which are the fruit of a plant in the gooseberry family.

dried fruit salad commonly made with tropical fruit like paw paw, pineapple and mango.

dried lavender available at specialist cooking stores.

dried mixed berries lightly crunchy dehydrated form of strawberries, blueberries, cherries. They can be eaten as is or used as an ingredient in cooking.

dried rose buds available at specialist cooking stores.

dried rose petals slightly chewy, dehydrated rose petals.

eggs if recipes call for raw or barely cooked eggs; exercise caution if there is a salmonella problem in your area.

ferrero raffaello is a crispy, creamy almond and coconut bite-sized sweet.

flour

plain an all-purpose wheat flour.

rice very fine, powdery, gluten-free flour; made from ground white rice.

self-raising plain flour with baking powder in the proportion of 1 cup flour to 2 teaspoons baking powder.

wholemeal plain also known as wholewheat flour; milled with the wheatgerm so is higher in fibre and more nutritious than plain flour.

food colouring vegetable-based substances available in liquid, paste or gel form.

frangelico an Italian liqueur flavoured with hazelnuts and spices.

fruit mince also called mince meat; a sweet mixture of dried fruits, sugar, suet, nuts and flavourings.

gelatine we used powdered gelatine.

ginger

fresh also called green or root ginger; the thick gnarled root of a tropical plant. Can be kept, peeled, covered with dry sherry in a jar and refrigerated, or frozen in an airtight container.

glacé fresh ginger root preserved in sugar syrup; crystallised ginger can be substituted if rinsed with warm water and dried before use.

wine made with a grape base to which ginger, spices, herbs and fruits have been added.

glacé cherries also called candied cherries; boiled in heavy sugar syrup and then dried.

glacé pineapple pineapple cooked in heavy sugar syrup then dried.

glucose syrup also called liquid glucose; a sugary syrup made from starches such as wheat and corn.

golden syrup a by-product of refined sugarcane; pure maple syrup or honey can be substituted.

grand marnier a brandy-based orange-flavoured liqueur.

hard caramels confectionery item made from sugar, glucose, condensed milk, flour, oil and gelatine.

hazelnuts also known as filberts; plump, grape-size, rich, sweet nut having a brown inedible skin that is removed by rubbing heated nuts together vigorously in a tea towel.

meal also called ground hazelnuts.

hundreds and thousands tiny sugar-syrup-coated sugar crystals that come in a variety of colours.

instant latte sachets caffè latte-flavoured milk powder made by Nestle. Available from supermarkets.

jelly crystals a combination of sugar, gelatine, colours and flavours; when dissolved in water it sets as firm jelly.

kahlua coffee-flavoured liqueur made in Mexico.

lemon-flavoured spread a ready-made lemon curd or lemon butter.

lemon grass a tall, clumping, lemon-smelling and tasting, sharp-edged aromatic tropical grass; the white lower part of the stem is used, finely chopped. Can be found, fresh, dried, powdered and frozen, in supermarkets, greengrocers and Asian food shops.

macadamias native to Australia, a rich and buttery nut; store in the refrigerator due to its high oil content.

macaroons a chewy biscuit made with egg white, sugar and coconut or almond meal.

madeira cake similar to pound cake, the top is sprinkled with candied lemon peel halfway through baking.

malibu a coconut-flavoured rum.

malted milk powder a blend of milk powder and malted cereal extract.

maltesers crispy malt balls covered in milk chocolate.

mandarin also called tangerine; a small, loose-skinned, easy-to-peel, sweet and juicy citrus fruit, prized for eating more than for juicing.

maple-flavoured syrup made from sugar cane rather than maple-tree sap; used in cooking or as a topping but cannot be considered an exact substitute for pure maple syrup.

maple syrup distilled from the sap of maple trees found only in Canada and parts of North America. Maple-flavoured syrup is not an adequate substitute for the real thing.

marsala a sweet fortified wine originally from Sicily.

marshmallows made from sugar, glucose, gelatine and cornflour.

marzipan a paste made from ground almonds, sugar and water. Similar to almond paste but sweeter, more pliable and finer in texture. Easily coloured and rolled into thin sheets.

milk we used full-cream homogenised milk unless otherwise specified.

buttermilk sold in the refrigerated dairy sections in supermarkets; is commercially made similarly to yogurt.

sweetened condensed a canned milk product consisting of milk with more than half the water content removed and sugar added to the milk that remains.

top 'n' fill a canned milk product made of condensed milk that has been boiled to a caramel.

mixed dried fruit commonly a combination of sultanas, raisins, currants, mixed peel and cherries.

mixed spice a blend of ground spices usually consisting of cinnamon, allspice and nutmeg.

nutmeg the dried nut of a tree native to Indonesia; is available ground or grate it fresh with a fine grater.

oatbran the hard and rather woody protective outer coating of oats which serves to protect the grain before it germinates.

pecans native to the United States and now grown locally; golden-brown, buttery and rich in flavour.

peppermint crisp chocolate bars crunchy peppermint toffee covered in chocolate.

pistachios green, delicately flavoured nuts inside hard off-white shells. Available salted or unsalted in their shells; you can also buy them shelled.

poppy seeds possessing a nutty, slightly sweet flavour and a dark blue-grey colour, come from capsules inside an opium plant.

prepared fondant also known as soft icing and ready-to-roll.

quince yellow-skinned fruit with hard texture and astringent, tart taste; eaten cooked or as a preserve.

rhubarb a plant with long, green-red stalks; become sweet and edible when cooked.

Rice Bubbles also known as Rice Krispies; a puffed rice grain cereal.

rind also known as zest.

rolled barley sliced barley kernels rolled flat into flakes.

rolled oats flattened oat grain rolled into flakes; traditionally used for porridge. Use traditional, not quick-cooking, oats in baking.

rose water extract made from crushed rose petals; used for its aromatic quality in many desserts.

savoiardi sponge finger biscuits also known as savoy biscuits or ladyfingers; Italian-style crisp biscuits made from a sponge-cake mixture.

semolina coarsely ground flour milled from durum wheat.

sesame snaps sesame seeds set in honey-toffee; sold in thin bar-shapes and available at supermarkets.

star fruit also known as carambola, five-corner fruit or Chinese star fruit.

sugar

brown a soft, fine granulated sugar containing molasses for its colour.

caster also called superfine or finely granulated table sugar.

demerara small-grained, golden-coloured crystal sugar.

icing also called confectioners' sugar or powdered sugar; crushed granulated sugar with added cornflour.

palm also called nam tan pip, jaggery, jawa or gula melaka; made from the sap of the sugar palm tree. Light brown to black in colour and usually sold in rock-hard cakes; use brown sugar if hard to find.

pure icing also called confectioners' sugar or powdered sugar.

vanilla is granulated or caster sugar flavoured with vanilla bean.

white coarse and granulated; also known as table sugar.

sugar-free fruit drops individually wrapped fruit-flavoured hard lollies made with artificial sweetener.

vanilla

bean dried long, thin pod from a tropical golden orchid; the minuscule black seeds inside the bean impart a distinctively sweet vanilla flavour.

extract vanilla beans that have been submerged in alcohol. Vanilla essence is not a suitable substitute.

violet crumble a honeycomb bar coated in milk chocolate.

wheat germ is the embryo of the wheat kernel, separated before milling for use as a vitamin-rich cereal or food supplement.

yogurt we use plain yogurt unless otherwise specified.

conversion chart

measures

One Australian metric measuring cup holds approximately 250ml; one Australian metric tablespoon holds 20ml; one Australian metric teaspoon holds 5ml.

The difference between one country's measuring cups and another's is within a two- or three-teaspoon variance, and will not affect your cooking results. North America, New Zealand and the United Kingdom use a 15ml tablespoon.

All cup and spoon measurements are level. The most accurate way of measuring dry ingredients is to weigh them. When measuring liquids, use a clear glass or plastic jug with the metric markings.

We use large eggs with an average weight of 60g.

dry measures

METRIC	IMPERIAL
15g	½oz
30g	1oz
60g	2oz
90g	3oz
125g	4oz (¼lb)
155g	5oz
185g	6oz
220g	7oz
250g	8oz (½lb)
280g	9oz
315g	10oz
345g	11oz
375g	12oz (¾lb)
410g	13oz
440g	14oz
470g	15oz
500g	16oz (1lb)
750g	24oz (1½lb)
1kg	32oz (2lb)

liquid measures

METRIC	IMPERIAL
30ml	1 fluid oz
60ml	2 fluid oz
100ml	3 fluid oz
125ml	4 fluid oz
150ml	5 fluid oz (¼ pint/1 gill)
190ml	6 fluid oz
250ml	8 fluid oz
300ml	10 fluid oz (½ pint)
500ml	16 fluid oz
600ml	20 fluid oz (1 pint)
1000ml (1 litre)	1¾ pints

length measures

3mm	⅛in
6mm	¼in
1cm	½in
2cm	¾in
2.5cm	1in
5cm	2in
6cm	2½in
8cm	3in
10cm	4in
13cm	5in
15cm	6in
18cm	7in
20cm	8in
23cm	9in
25cm	10in
28cm	11in
30cm	12in (1ft)

oven temperatures

These oven temperatures are only a guide for conventional ovens. For fan-forced ovens, check the manufacturer's manual.

	°C (CELSIUS)	°F (FAHRENHEIT)	GAS MARK
Very slow	120	250	½
Slow	150	275-300	1-2
Moderately slow	160	325	3
Moderate	180	350-375	4-5
Moderately hot	200	400	6
Hot	220	425-450	7-8
Very hot	240	475	9

index